The Art of Playing the Recorder

The Art of Playing the Recorder

Daniel Waitzman

AMS PRESS

NEW YORK

FIRST AMS EDITION, 1978

Library of Congress Cataloging in Publication Data

Waitzman, Daniel.
    The art of playing the recorder.

    1. Recorder (Musical instrument)—Instruction and
study. I. Title.
MT340.W25   788'.53'0712   77-78321
ISBN 0-404-16010-7
ISBN 0-404-16011-5 pbk.

"A musician cannot move others unless he too is moved."

C.P.E. Bach, *Essay on the True Art of Playing
Keyboard Instruments,* trans. by William J.
Mitchell (New York, 1949), p. 152.

"We shall now investigate the principal qualities of good execution in general. Good execution must be first of all *true
and distinct.* Not only must each note be heard, but each
note must be sounded with its true intonation, so that all will
be intelligible to the listener. Not one must be left out. You
must try to make each sound as beautiful as possible."

Johann Joachim Quantz, *Essay of a Method for
Playing the Transverse Flute,* trans. by Edward R.
Reilly (New York, 1966), p. 122.

Contents

Preface

This little book is intended as a broad overview of the basic techniques of recorder-playing. It is not a "method," in the conventional sense. Although written mainly with the serious student in mind, it is hoped that it will be read by all who are interested in the recorder, and that it will contribute to the enjoyment of the recorder by amateurs, as well as to a better understanding of the instrument by aspiring professionals. It is intended to supplement, rather than to replace, private instruction. There is *no* substitute for the guidance of a good teacher. Only a teacher can respond to the needs of the individual student and provide a living example of the precepts of musicianship in action. Only a teacher can communicate those vital principles too subtle to be expressed in words. Those who assert the contrary fool only themselves and others who are ignorant of the difficulties attending the mastery of a musical instrument, even under ideal conditions.

No instrument is more misunderstood than the recorder. Though surely the most popular woodwind, in terms of sheer numbers of instruments made, bought, and—after a fashion—played, only a handful of musicians know how to make it sound like a real musical instrument. Moreover, the recorder was as misunderstood in the eighteenth century as it is today. Eighteenth-century recorder technique was at least one hundred years behind the times, as compared with eighteenth-century flute technique. Consequently, the old books on re-

corder technique are mainly of historical interest—in sharp
contrast to old treatises on the techniques of other instruments, whose pre-twentieth-century practitioners were far in
advance of their recorder-playing colleagues. It is a mistake to
assume, from the superb achievements of eighteenth-century
flutists, harpsichordists, and string players, that eighteenth-
century recorderists were equally competent, particularly in
view of the recorder's inferior status as a doubler's instrument in those days. In some ways, the eighteenth century
was no different from our own time—and from other centuries as well. It was a time of contradictions, imperfections,
and inconsistencies, besides being one of unsurpassed musical
excellence. Human nature remains the same over the biologi-
cally brief time span of a few centuries.

Most modern books on recorder-playing are written on a
very elementary level, for amateur use. Their treatment of
the subject tends to be cursory and superficial. Even the
more rigorous works tend to contain numerous errors, despite
their many perceptive insights. Either they fail to take into
account advances made in recorder technique since the eighteenth century—particularly in the last eleven years—or else
they confine themselves to non-melodic, "avant-garde" techniques necessary for the performance of what might be called
post-musical or para-musical art forms, in which subtle refine-
ments of tone quality, inspired by and derived from bel-canto
vocal styles, are of minimal importance. The problem of raising traditional, melodically-oriented recorder technique up to
the level of mid-eighteenth-century flute technique has, it
would seem, been deliberately ignored, as being contrary to
the prevailing ideology of the "recorder movement," or perhaps as having no "practical" utility, in view of the limited
technical demands made by the traditional repertoire. This
attitude ignores not only the value of post-eighteenth-century
techniques in facilitating a more *musically* authentic perform-

ance of this repertoire, but also the value of technical development and study for its own sake. In addition, it fails to take
into account the very practical application of these techniques
in arrangements of older music (for which there is ample
precedent in pre-nineteenth-century musical practices), in
newly-composed melodic music, and, indeed, even in "avant-
garde" non-melodic styles.

This book attempts to remedy this state of affairs. It
examines the elements of recorder technique, as they apply
to both the bell-keyed recorder and to the conventional keyless recorder. Its approach is artistic, rather than scientific, in
that I do not claim objective validity for all of the assertions
made herein. It confines itself to the concert recorder—the
"alto in f'"—since this represents the basic form of instrument
from the player's viewpoint, just as the concert transverse
flute in c', rather than the piccolo or the alto flute, is of paramount importance in the study of the transverse flute.[1] Mastery of the concert recorder virtually assures mastery of the
other sizes as well. Furthermore, this book excludes all techniques not needed for the performance of tonal, vocally-
oriented music, although the matters discussed in it have obvious implications for those interested in cultivating the recorder as an instrument of "avant-garde" compositional styles. It
is, in short, intended as an approximation of the sort of work
that might have been written in the mid- to late eighteenth
century, had the recorder's resources been more thoroughly
explored in those days.

This work makes almost no mention of the purely musical aspects of performance, partly because the subject has
already been covered in depth by the old treatises, and partly

---

[1] The designation "concert recorder" in no way implies that the other sizes of recorder are unsuited for use in public performance.

because the advent of the phonograph[2] and the emergence of a viable neo-baroque school of performance have, to a large extent, rendered the production of newly-written treatises on interpretation largely superfluous. There exist today a number of performers who have successfully re-created eighteenth-century traditions of performance, with no apologies necessary. To be sure, a time-machine visit to eighteenth-century musical cultures would probably result in some surprises; but *the essential life of the old traditions has been restored*—and this is what counts. It is suggested that differences among eighteenth-century musicians would very possibly be as substantial as those between eighteenth-century musicians and some of their twentieth-century counterparts. For a discussion of purely musical questions, the reader is referred to the fine eighteenth-century treatises on the subject—particularly to Quantz's *Essay*.[3] This monumental treatise remains an inspiration to us all, not because it is old or "authentic," but because it is so superb and musicianly.

My well-known advocacy of the bell-keyed recorder has occasioned a bit of controversy, most of it quite unnecessary. The bell-keyed recorder is neither perfect nor modern; but it does represent the closest approach to technical perfection yet achieved in recorder design—which is not saying very much. It constitutes an *evolutionary*, rather than a *revolutionary*, change, but a significant one nonetheless. At the time that the bulk of the present work was written, it appeared that a line of rationally-constructed bell-keyed recorders

---

[2] In lieu of a chapter on musical performance in the present book, and also as an illustration of the application of some of the techniques discussed herein, I cite my recent recording of a Telemann C Major Sonata, performed on bell-keyed recorder, on a Musical Heritage Society disc (*Eighteenth-Century Flute Music*, catalogue no. MHS 1860, available by mail from the Musical Heritage Society, Inc., 14 Park Road, Tinton Falls, New Jersey 07724).

[3] Johann Joachim Quantz, *Essay of a Method for Playing the Transverse Flute*, trans. by Edward R. Reilly (New York: The Free Press, 1966). (Originally published as *Versuch einer Anweisung die Flöte traversiere zu Spielen*, Berlin, 1752.)

would be manufactured for the first time. That this has not come about reflects on the present state of recorder-playing, rather than on the inherent viability of the bell-keyed recorder. Music history, like history in general, does not always follow the ideal path: witness the extinction of the wide-bore Quantz-type flute, the long eclipse of the harpsichord—and the apparent demise, even at the moment of its birth, of the specially-tuned bell-keyed recorder. Although this book is probably the instrument's epitaph, I still hope that it may someday influence instrument makers to pursue the subject once again. The recorder cannot survive as anything more than a folk instrument unless good instruments become available. Those now available serve well enough for amateur use; but they are almost all unfit for serious study. The discussion of recorder design in Chapter I sets forth, for the first time, the rationale for the tuning of a well-made bell-keyed recorder; some of the other material in this chapter appeared in the English *Recorder & Music Magazine* for September 1969 (Vol. 3, No. 3), and is included here with the kind permission of the editor of that issue, Ronald E. Corcoran.

In view of the precarious situation of the recorder today, and particularly of the difficulty in finding a good instrument, it is recommended that the serious student study another instrument at some point in his career—the earlier the better. A logical choice is the newly-revived conical Boehm transverse flute (now being manufactured again in the United States by the brothers Bickford and Robert Brannen, of Littleton Road, Harvard, Massachusetts 01451), since it embodies much of the recorder's tone quality and articulation sensitivity. Indeed, every recorderist should learn to play the flute, since recorder and transverse flute are but different versions of the same instrument. A well-played recorder should sound much like a well-played flute. There should be no essential difference between the modes of expression considered proper for the two instruments. The recorder has the edge in its ability to articulate precisely and to negotiate rapid leaps, and in its distinctively expressive upper middle range; however, its dynamic range is small and its powers of legato more difficult to employ than those of the flute. Its most effective tessitura is also too high, when compared with that of the concert flute. The flute has a wider dynamic range and a more facile legato than the recorder; but it is distinctly inferior to the recorder in crispness of articulation as well as in purity and intensity of tone. Both instruments are as difficult to master; however, recorder technique is more cumbersome than flute technique. Both recorderist and transverse flutist must try to overcome the respective defects inherent in the two types of flute. The sensitive recorderist tries to make his instrument sing like a well-played transverse flute; the wise flutist takes as his model the well-focused, sharply-articulated sound of a well-played recorder.

The reader should be warned that any attempt to codify the procedures of playing an instrument inevitably results in some distortion. Thus, the techniques discussed on the following pages may seem mechanical and—in the pejorative sense of the term—artificial. In a sense, every printed statement is a lie. The reader must always make an effort to overcome the deficiencies of verbal communication in order to understand the true nature of the matters under discussion, so that he may assimilate them into his own knowledge. He should also recognize the possibility that some of the techniques discussed below may have to be modified to accommodate the individual. For example, those who find it physically impossible to master the type of double-tonguing which I prefer, or the hand position which I advocate, should feel free to do what works best for them and feels most comfortable, whether or not it conforms to my instructions—as long as it enables them to achieve the desired results. For, as another writer on the subject observed many generations ago, "You must always follow what seems most natural."[4]

I wish to thank my teachers, colleagues, and students, who have all contributed in one way or another to my understanding and formulation of the subject of this book. I should also acknowledge my deep indebtedness to the classical writers on flute-playing, whose works stand as models of excellence and of methodology for those who attempt to write about the art of playing the recorder.

Daniel Waitzman
Flushing, New York

March, 1977

[4] Jacques Hotteterre le Romain, *Principles of the Flute, Recorder & Oboe*, trans. and ed. by David Lasocki (London: Barrie & Rockliff, The Crescent Press, 1968), p. 38. (Originally published as *Principes de la Flute Traversiere, ou Flute d'Allemagne, de la Flute à Bec, ou Flute Douce, et du Haut-Bois*, Paris, 1707.)

EXPLANATION OF SYMBOLS AND DEFINITION
OF TERMS NOT EXPLAINED IN THE TEXT

Pitches are indicated in the customary fashion:

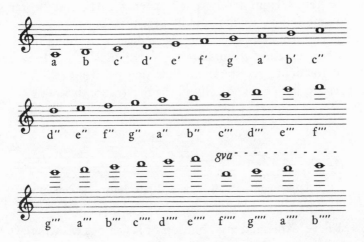

The term "register" corresponds roughly with the acoustical terms "harmonic" or "mode." It denotes specific sections of the recorder's compass, each of which is produced by a particular vibrational mode of the air column. For example, the first or low register, extending from f' to normally-fingered g", consists entirely of fundamentals. The second register, encompassing the notes g" through d''' on the keyless recorder, involves one degree of overblowing. The third register, for the production of which the air column over-blows two degrees, includes the traditional fingerings for the notes e♭‴ through f‴. At least nine registers may be distin-guished, of which the first five are of paramount importance. The transition from one register to another in slurred pas-sages almost always involves a more or less obtrusive click. Fortunately the registers of the recorder overlap to a great degree, particularly on the bell-keyed recorder, permitting the player to avoid most of the more objectionable breaks through the proper selection of duplicate fingerings.

I have used the terms "range" and "registers" to refer loosely to general areas of the recorder's compass. The low range of the concert recorder coincides with the first register and extends from f′ to first-register g″. The middle range (also referred to as the middle registers) runs from second-register g″ to about g‴. The high range (also called the high registers) extends from about g‴ through c⁗. The acute range (or acute registers) extends upward from c♯⁗. These ranges are shown graphically in the illustration below:

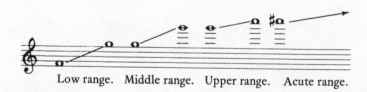

Low range.   Middle range.   Upper range.   Acute range.

I have explained my notation of fingerings elsewhere (pp. 80-81); but for the convenience of the reader, this explanation is repeated below. The holes of the recorder to be closed for each fingering are indicated by numbers. The holes of the re-corder are numbered 1 through 8, starting with the thumb-hole. X indicates the closing of the bell by means of the bell key, or, in the case of the keyless recorder (and on the bell-keyed recorder when the right-hand little finger is otherwise occupied, unless the instrument is equipped with a long bell key for the little finger of the left hand), by the pressing of the bell against the knee. A line under a numeral or under X indicates partial covering of the hole in question, in order to form a speaker-vent (see Chapter V). This is called pinching in the case of hole 1, and half-holing in the case of the remaining holes. The definitions of these symbols are summarized below:

Pinching:

<u>1</u> Pinching, type unspecified. (To be read as "one pinched.")

1' First-position or upper-crescent pinching. (To be read as "one first-position pinched," or "one upper-crescent pinched.")

1" Second-position or double-crescent pinching. (To be read as "one second-position pinched, or "one double-crescent pinched.")

1 Half-position pinching (to be read as "one half-position pinched," or "one half-pinched.")

Half-holing:

<u>2</u> (To be read as "two half-holed," or "half-holing on two.")

Half-stopping:

A fraction to the left of a number indicates partial stopping of the hole in question; e.g.:

½7 (To ,be read as "one-half seven," or "seven half-stopped." (For an explanation of the distinction between half-holing and half-stopping, see p. 65.)

0 All holes uncovered.

It is with some reluctance that I have decided to refer to the subject of this book as "the recorder," in accordance with common usage. In the instrument's last pre-twentieth century days as an important woodwind, it was known as "the flute"—a far more accurate description, but one that would today cause endless confusion with the transverse flute. It has been proposed to call it "the blockflute," which would make perfect musical sense, besides eliminating any confusion with the magnetic tape recorder. The term "recorder" had fallen into disuse as early as the seventeenth century; it was revived by gentlemen dilettantes who sought refuge in the trappings of preciousness and obscurity, not by professional musicians. The damage has been done, however; and it would probably take an act of Congress and a major advertising campaign to set things right. The recorder it is, then. "A *flauto* by any other name sounds just as *dolce*."

However, I have taken the liberty of referring to the soprano and sopranino recorders as "piccolo recorders." The use of this term clears up much confusion among conductors and other non-recorder-playing musicians, who might otherwise be unaware that some of the most beautiful works of the piccolo repertoire were intended for recorder, rather than for the transverse piccolo. To avoid confusing the recorder-playing reader, I have usually retained the customary terminology in parentheses.

THE ART
OF PLAYING THE RECORDER

CHAPTER I

The Qualities Required
of a Good Concert Recorder

GENERAL OBSERVATIONS

The selection of a good concert recorder is a matter of utmost importance. Only a first-class instrument is suitable for serious work at the advanced level; anything less is worthless. "Second best," as far as recorders are concerned, is very bad indeed. Good instruments are almost impossible to obtain. Here, as in other aspects of the recorder world, mediocrity or worse is the rule, and excellence the exception.

It is customary, at the present time, to distinguish three broad categories of recorder: Renaissance, baroque, and neo-baroque. The Renaissance model follows more or less the pattern of the sixteenth- and early seventeenth-century recorders, sacrificing compass, flexibility, and agility in order to gain volume in the low register. Despite its acknowledged value for the performance of Renaissance music, its limitations disqualify it from consideration here. The term "baroque recorder" actually includes a considerable variety of late seventeenth- and eighteenth-century designs, some better than others.

Recently, some makers have begun building instruments purporting to be "replicas" of eighteenth-century recorders. These vary considerably in quality and utility. Most of these so-called replicas exhibit modern features to varying degrees, and thus fall under the classification of "neo-baroque," rather than "baroque." The term "neo-baroque" designates the recorder now in general use, which, though patterned after baroque examples, incorporates certain contemporary modifications, the most important of which is the "English fingering" for the $B^\flat$'s in the first two octaves.[1] Most of the other differences between "baroque" and "neo-baroque" recorders represent differences in detail, rather than in principle, at least from the player's viewpoint. Hence, they may be ignored for our purposes. The distinction between the two categories, questionable to begin with, is in any case of diminishing significance, in view of recent developments in recorder making. Not only have recorder makers produced baroque "replicas" with modern features; some have begun to re-incorporate several of the desirable characteristics of baroque designs into their neo-baroque instruments. For present purposes, any post-Renaissance recorder with "English fingering" will be classified under the heading, "neo-baroque." The absence of this feature must be considered a defect. The baroque tuning of the $B^\flat$'s resulted in needless fingering difficulties, and cannot be justified on rational grounds. The combination of baroque fingering and bell key would be most awkward, since the former requires the frequent closure of the eighth hole by the same finger which usually controls the key.

Despite the excellence of a few surviving eighteenth-century recorders, there seems no reason to believe, as some do, that the neo-baroque recorder is inherently inferior to its baroque prototype. Those who attempt to prove such inferi-

[1] See pp. 82 and 90.

ority by comparing the best surviving baroque recorders with the worst mass-produced contemporary instruments only confuse the issue.

A fourth category of recorder—the "modern recorder"—has yet to be developed. The lack of such an instrument, which would incorporate advances in woodwind technology made since the eighteenth century, makes it all the more incumbent upon recorderists to realize all the potentials of the existing ultra-conservative models with which they must work. At the same time, it should cause the open-minded musician to marvel over the awesome fact that an instrument technologically as "primitive" as the one-keyed flute and the two-keyed oboe has managed to hold its own among Boehm flute, Triébert oboe, and Heckel bassoon.

This book concerns itself with the neo-baroque concert recorder, as defined above. Within this broad category, one may, for practical purposes, distinguish among three types of instrument:

1. The *keyless recorder,* also called the normal, ordinary, or conventional recorder.

2. The compromise bell-keyed recorder, hereafter referred to as the *compromise recorder.* This is basically an ordinary recorder to which a bell key has been added as an auxiliary device, with the aim of incorporating many of the advantages conferred by the bell key while retaining all the conventional fingerings of the keyless recorder. It may or may not exhibit some of the modifications characteristic of the true bell-keyed recorder, provided that these do not interfere with the normal fingerings in any way.

3. The true bell-keyed recorder, henceforth called the *bell-keyed recorder.* This type departs from conventional recorder design in certain important details, in order to exploit to the fullest extent the additional fingerings provided by the key, even at the expense of the intonation and timbre of certain traditional fingerings. On this instrument, the bell key functions as an integral, rather than as an auxiliary, device.

These distinctions are neither absolute, nor, despite their practical importance, are they indicative of fundamental differences in design (such as those existing between the French and the German bassoon, for example). Some compromise recorders exhibit, to varying degrees, features normally associated with bell-keyed recorders. Some ostensibly normal recorders are in reality identical to bell-keyed recorders, except for the absence of a bell key. I myself played on such an instrument for years before having it fitted with a bell key. Nevertheless, despite their subtlety, the differences among the three types of recorder assume vital importance in the study of recorder technique. In view of this fact, an examination of these differences seems in order. It will be preceded by a summary of the desiderata common to all three types of neo-baroque concert recorder.

Ideally, all three types of recorder ought to sound with the loudest, freest tone possible, consistent with good tone quality. The tone should be well focused throughout the entire melodic range, with a minimum of hiss or noise. It should be flexible and creamy, rather than brittle and choked, allowing rapid articulation and maximum dynamic and tonal inflection. Far too many recorders exhibit excessive reediness and inflexibility; these qualities constitute poor substitutes for true resonance, with which they are all too often confused. Such instruments may be relatively easy for the inexperienced player to control; but their expressive range is unduly limited. Register breaks—particularly the break between conventionally-fingered d''' and e'''—ought to be as unobtrusive as possible. The instrument ought to be free from wolf notes —i.e., unstable tones that tend to burble. However, some otherwise excellent recorders have wolf notes on g' and/or f#'. In some cases, these may be eliminated (as, for example, by removal of varnish from the sharp edge of the lip with acetone); but since their elimination frequently results in injury to the third octave and intensification of the above-mentioned d'''-e''' register break, some players may prefer to tolerate them.

In the low register, the tone should be neither excessively reedy nor overly weak and colorless, but round and somewhat fluty, with a slight edge. It should be possible to sound a′ with a very firm, loud, and reedy tone. As one ascends into the higher registers, the tone should become gradually rounder, fuller, and more flexible. It should, however, be possible to play into the third octave without increase in volume or loss of focus, and with only a relatively slight increase in breath pressure.

Since recorder voicing is largely a matter of individual taste, and since the voicing may change as a result of use, a good maker should be willing and able to revoice a recorder to suit the player's personal taste.

All standard and duplicate fingerings, including second-register g″ and cross-fingered a″, should be in tune, except as noted below in the individual discussions of each of the three types of neo-baroque concert recorder. On all three types of recorder, a′, and, to a slight extent, g♯′, b♭′, and b′ should be tuned slightly flat, in relation to their octaves, so that they may be blown more strongly.[2] However, c″ should be in tune with its octave, c‴.

The list of materials suitable for use in the manufacture of first-class recorders is extensive. It includes a wide variety of woods, as well as ivory. Unfortunately, recorder makers have yet to experiment with tubes of ebonite (which Rockstro considered the most suitable material for transverse flutes)[3] or fine gauge silver. The relatively high quality of some cheap, mass-produced plastic recorders raises the question of whether certain kinds of plastic might not lend themselves to use for first-class, hand-made instruments. Whether or not any synthetic material or silver might ultimately compete with wood can only be ascertained by open-minded experimentation. Be this as it may, it seems clear that the influence of the material

[2] *Cf.* Quantz's advice on the tuning of the octaves on the eighteenth century transverse flute, in Quantz, *On Playing the Flute,* p. 55.

[3] Richard Shepherd Rockstro, *A Treatise on the Flute* (2nd ed., London: 1928. Facsimile ed., London: Musica Rara, 1967), pp. 145-147.

of the instrument on tone and response, though significant, must be considered far less important than the quality of workmanship and design.

The bore of a recorder ought to be, but almost never is, finished with the same care customarily devoted to the exterior of the instrument. "It is a point of honour with the best makers to finish the bore with the greatest care, leaving it not only exactly dimensioned but with a mirror-like polish."[4] Under no circumstances should it be perforated by pillars or other supports for keywork or thumbrest, as is too often the case.

In order to minimize the gap in the bore at the juncture of headjoint and center-piece, which results when one tunes the recorder downward, it is advantageous to glue the cork to the concave surface of the joint (as was formerly done by at least one maker), rather than to a recessed band cut into the circumference of the tenon (as is the usual practice). This unorthodox construction enables the tenon to be made as thin as possible, so that it may better fulfill its function as a tuning joint.

The lowest two fingerholes should always be double holes, to facilitate the production of the lowest semitones.

The mechanical design of the recorder's mouthpiece is badly in need of reform, since it makes little provision for adjustment, tends to get out of order, and discourages easy access and proper maintenance. Some of the best recorder makers glue a strip of cork to a recessed band cut into the circumference of the block, to facilitate its easy removal and replacement. It is far better for the block to be loose than for it to be excessively tight. The block, being made of soft, absorbent wood, tends to swell; if fitted too tightly, it can easily crack the mouthpiece. To prevent this, the mouthpiece is

---

[4] F. Geoffrey Rendall, *The Clarinet* (2nd ed., rev.; London: Ernest Benn Ltd., 1957, p. 44.

often jacketed with ivory; this, however, may also crack as a result of the block's expansion.

Having summarized the desiderata shared by all three types of neo-baroque concert recorder, let us now consider each type separately.

THE BELL-KEYED RECORDER

On the bell-keyed recorder, the following fingerings should be in tune (except as noted), and of good quality:

b″ 12345(7)X.
c#‴ 1235X.
d‴ 123X.
d#‴ 123(5)67.
e‴ 123567X. Usually sharp, unfortunately.
f‴ 12567X.
g‴ 12457. Also 1″24X.
a‴ 1346½7X.
b♭‴ 123(5)6X.
b‴ 1″2357.

In order that the fingerings given above for c#‴, d‴, and certain other notes may be in tune, it appears, unfortunately, that the following conventional fingerings must be out of tune, as noted:

d″ 123. Slightly sharp.
d#″ 1245. Slightly flat.
c#‴ 1235. Very flat.
d‴ 123. Flat.
e‴ 123356. Slightly flat.
f‴ 1256. Flat.
g#‴ 134. Slightly flat.

These fingerings require adjustment by the player, except when used in fast passages. (The techniques for adjusting them will be discussed in a later chapter.)

In voicing a bell-keyed recorder, one should favor the middle and high registers, while striving for maximum dynamic and tonal flexibility. It should be possible to swell d''', e''', and f''', when fingered with the key, as well as other notes, without the tone becoming impure. One ought to be able to play all the notes up to and including b''', at a mezzo-piano. The instrument should play chromatically up through d'''' without the necessity of shading the window. The first note of a well-made bell-keyed recorder to show serious deterioration in tone quality, as one ascends into the third octave, is c''''. c#'''', d'''', e'''', and f'''' should be obtainable, although not necessarily pleasant.

Despite the above-mentioned favoring of the upper registers, the low register should not be neglected. In addition to the general requirements for this register mentioned earlier in this chapter, it is necessary that the following fingerings be loud, reedy, and stable:

c''   1234X. Also 12348.
d''   1236(½)7X.
d#'' 12467½8.
e''   126.

The skillful use of these and similar reinforcement fingerings enables a knowledgeable player to compensate for the bell-keyed recorder's slight inherent weakness in the low register, in comparison with a keyless recorder of equal quality.

The short bell key for the little finger of the right-hand may be considered standard. The long key for the left-hand little finger recommends itself only as a *second* key, to eliminate completely the use of the knee to close the bell (as when fingering alternate c''''=123578X), and to make available additional fingering combinations, particularly those involving both the closing of the bell and the eighth hole. Its design poses many problems, which must be overcome before this key becomes a standard accessory. The short key's touch should be conveniently placed to permit the little finger to slide from the key to the eighth hole, in one motion. Its action should be light, free from rebound, and quiet. Unfortunately, the proximity of the pad to the bell exercises an adverse effect on the intonation and timbre of certain notes, particularly third register e''' and f'''.[5] Since these notes are already compromised on a well-designed bell-keyed recorder, it is essential that this effect be minimized through careful design of the key. A bell key must have an airtight seal; otherwise it is all but worthless. The quality, response, and intonation of many notes depend upon this. To facilitate the realization of these and other desiderata, it is desirable that the key, or at least its lower section, be mounted on pillars.

To test a bell key's closure, one fingers the double-stop a'''-g''' (23467X), with only light pressure on the key. If the pad does not seal properly, only the a''' will sound. Proper closure may be facilitated by wrapping one or more sheets of plastic kitchen wrap around pad and cup, and securing them with transparent tape.

Rationale for the Tuning of the Bell-Keyed Recorder

Since d''' has a brighter, more open sound, as well as a greater dynamic range and ease of speech, when fingered with the bell closed (123X), it is advantageous to be able to finger it in this manner without its being sharp, as it would be on the conventionally-tuned recorder. Once this fingering for d''' is accepted as normal, it becomes desirable to have c#''', the leading tone of D major, in tune when made with the bell closed (1235X), in order to avoid a register break between it and d'''. (The abandonment of the traditional fingering for c#'''—1235—as a normal fingering is not as much of a loss as it seems at first glance; this fingering is usually somewhat flat and slow to speak, even on the conventional recorder.) More-

---

[5] See Steven Silverstein's letter to the editor in *The American Recorder*, Vol. IX, No. 3 (Summer, 1968), p. 94.

over, the use of $\underline{1}2357X$, a variant of the new normal fingering for c#''', makes possible the elimination of the register
break between c#''' and d#''', c#''' and e''', and c#''' and f'''.
Similarly, the availability of $\underline{1}237X$, a variant of the new normal fingering for d''', enables one to slur from d''' to conventionally-fingered e''' without encountering the traditional
register break. (The felicitous elimination of these register
breaks results from the surprising fact that the new fingerings
for c#''' and d''' belong to the third register—as do those for
d#''' and conventionally-fingered e'''—rather than to the second register, like the traditional fingerings, which they appear
to resemble.) If, in addition, b'' is in tune when fingered
$\underline{1}2345(7)X$, certain passages are greatly facilitated, particularly those involving a#'', and/or the new fingerings for c#'''
and d''':

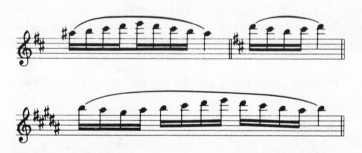

The new fingering for b'' also provides a stronger, more flexible alternative to the traditional cross-fingering. The require-
ment that g''' be in tune (rather than sharp, as is frequently
the case on keyless recorders) when fingered $\underline{1}2457$ stems
from the need to free the right-hand little finger from its
task of covering the eighth hole as much as possible, so that it
may be available to operate the key.

Some players may wonder why the deliberate flattening
of the second register should not be carried still further, in
order that c''' may be fingered uniformly with c#''', d''', and
alternate b''—i.e., with the bell closed, as $\underline{1}234X$. The answer,

of course, is that conventionally-fingered c''' leaves little to be desired in sonority, flexibility, or ease of production. It is, in fact, the highest second register tone of which this can be said. Moreover, as the tonic of the easiest major key of the recorder, and a note treated as the highest tone of the instrument's middle register in the days when much of the traditional repertoire was composed, it seems desirable that c''' remain in the second register, in order to facilitate legato passages. Aside from this, any attempt to flatten the second register further, in order to make 1234X the normal fingering for c''', would probably create serious difficulties by making the traditional fingerings for $c\sharp'''$ and d''' too flat to be used at all, and making even the bell-keyed fingerings for these notes uncomfortably flat.

THE KEYLESS RECORDER

On this instrument, the standard keyless fingerings should be in tune with a minimum of adjustment. In particular, the octaves d''-d''', e''-e''', and f''-f''' ought to be neither narrow (as on the bell-keyed recorder), nor wide (as on imperfectly constructed keyless recorders), but perfectly in tune. $c\sharp'''$ should be no more than slightly flat when fingered 1235. It is desirable, but not essential, that g''' be in tune, rather than sharp, when fingered 12457.

In voicing, the low and middle registers should be favored, and the notes above $g\sharp'''$ ignored. The quality and intonation of those fingerings in which the bell is closed may, of course, be ignored. However, the best keyless recorders can be made to play into the third octave with surprisingly little loss of quality, using fingerings normally associated with the bell-keyed and compromise recorders. Apparently, a good design assures a high degree of excellence over the entire range.

Since the keyless recorder's vocabulary of fingerings is comparatively limited, it is particularly important that the

register breaks between d''' and e''', and f''' and g''' be made
as unobtrusive as possible.

THE COMPROMISE RECORDER

In theory, this instrument should be bored, voiced, and
tuned exactly like the keyless recorder. In practice, it is desirable to have b'' fingered as 12345(7)X in tune, since the correct tuning of this fingering does not seem to detract from
any of the properties of the keyless instrument. Indeed, the
makers of all neo-baroque recorders, keyless or otherwise,
could render players a service by modifying their designs to
insure the correct intonation of this fingering, thereby pro-
viding for the possible addition of a bell key at some future
date.

Because of its nature, the compromise recorder may be
thought of as the least standardized of the three types of neo-
baroque concert recorder. The question of how far to go in
the direction of bell-keyed design must be decided by the
individual player and maker. The compromise recorder may
be voiced either like the keyless recorder, the true bell-keyed
recorder, or somewhere in between, depending on the use for
which it is intended. If the second course is followed, the
instrument will be almost as versatile as the bell-keyed recorder, while at the same time preserving the trueness of all
the traditional fingerings. However, the low register may suf-
fer some injury.

In designing the bell key for a compromise recorder, special care should usually be taken to maximize the distance
between pad and bell in open position, in order not to injure
the traditional fingerings—even if this impedes the action of
the key somewhat. Here again, the individual player and
maker may have to choose between perfect intonation and a
more efficient key.

THE ADVANTAGES AND DISADVANTAGES
OF EACH TYPE

Of the three types of neo-baroque recorder, the bell-keyed recorder is by far the most versatile, in terms of compass, dynamic range, tonal nuance, and the ability to negotiate relatively remote tonalities. Its melodic range extends from f' to c'''', while its complete range reaches upwards beyond f'''' (although most of the tones above f'''' are unstable, while most tones above c'''' are generally unsuitable for conventional stepwise melodic writing). This two-and-one-half-octave melodic range exceeds that of the keyless recorder by only a major third, at least in theory. In practice, however, the melodic capabilities of the bell-keyed recorder far exceed those of the keyless instrument. The melodic potential of the latter instrument's upper middle range (i.e., the notes between d''' and g#''' inclusive) is severely limited by numerous register breaks, fingering difficulties, and inequalities and deficiencies in tone, all of which may be largely circumvented on the bell-keyed recorder through the judicious combination of keyed and keyless fingerings. The new fingerings combine a greater dynamic range with an increased responsiveness. This last characteristic facilitates the attainment of a more perfect legato, by minimizing the obtrusiveness of register breaks. The availability of a whole new set of alternate fingerings greatly increases the instrument's coloristic and dynamic resources. The generally flatter tuning of the upper-middle range (the notes between c#''' and g''' inclusive) allows one to play louder than is possible on the keyless and compromise recorders, on which this part of the range tends to go sharp, unless played at a mezzo-piano. Since it is easier and more practical to sharpen a flat note than to lower a sharp one,[6] the player thereby gains a reserve of power with no sacrifice

[6] See p. 5, n. 2, above.

of pianissimo capabilities, and therefore, a widened dynamic range. Needless to say, he also acquires increased powers of projection as a result, although much depends on the qualities of one's individual instrument, in this respect.

This increase in versatility is not attained without cost, however. Although bell-keyed recorder technique represents an extension of keyless recorder technique (just as the technique of the eight-keyed flute grew out of that of the earlier, one-keyed instrument),[7] the bell-keyed recorder does demand greater effort from the player than the keyless instrument, particularly in fingering. Its fingerings are far more numerous than those of the ordinary recorder. Duplicate fingerings abound, forcing the player to decide among various combinations. One may have to use a different fingering for the same note depending on whether the passage in which it occurs ascends or descends, calls for slurring or tonguing, moves by step or by skip, or lies in one key or another. Some players will delight in this superabundance of fingerings, which constitutes one of the instrument's chief advantages over the keyless recorder. Others will find it disturbing. It certainly does not facilitate sight-reading.

Reference has already been made to the injury to the intonation of several of the bell-keyed recorder's keyless fingerings, resulting from the proper tuning of the keyed fingerings. Although the traditional fingerings remain available and essential on this instrument, they require that the player employ the appropriate techniques for the adjustment of their intonation. (It should be noted, however, that the keyless

---

[7] Excellent discussions of eight-keyed flute fingering may be found in Rockstro, pp. 299-303; 458-465; and in Johann Georg Tromlitz, *Ueber die Flöten mit mehren Klappen* (Leipzig: Adam Friedrich Böhme, 1800; facsimile ed. by Frits Knuf, Amsterdam, 1973). The fingering of the eight-keyed flute bears a remarkable resemblance to that of the bell-keyed recorder in principle, though not, of course, in substance. Both instruments employ a large vocabulary of fingerings; and both represent evolutionary outgrowths from baroque prototypes, which persist relatively unchanged, as the core of the newer instruments.

recorder reveals its full potential only when played by one familiar with these techniques.) With the assistance of these procedures, the player can even ignore the keyed fingerings altogether, gradually adding more of them to his fingering vocabulary, as he becomes more familiar with the instrument.[8]

Since the bell-keyed recorder is bored, tuned, and voiced to accommodate an extended compass, its low register is likely to be weaker than that of a well-made keyless recorder, at least in theory.[9] (In practice, this is not always the case, due to the availability of keyed reinforcement fingerings in the low register, as well as to the relatively inferior workmanship and design of most ordinary recorders in comparison with the few existing bell-keyed recorders, all of which have been built with professional use in mind.) In addition, certain keys, notably the important key of F minor, are more difficult and somewhat less satisfactory in some respects, due to complications resulting from the flatness of conventionally-fingered d♭''' and f'''. Finally, the key requires careful attention and occasional adjustment.

The compromise recorder offers some of the advantages of the bell-keyed recorder without injury to the keyless fingerings, or, in most cases, to the low register. Its melodic range may be as great as that of the bell-keyed instrument. However, since some of the keyed fingerings are out of tune, and because the voicing is usually that of the normal recorder, the compromise recorder cannot quite equal the bell-keyed recorder in versatility. It tends, like the keyless recorder, to be somewhat softer than the bell-keyed instrument, except in the low register. The compromise recorder recommends itself primarily to more conservative players, who wish to realize

---

[8] See above, p. 4.

[9] The modern Boehm flute offers another example of an instrument on which the low register has been injured in order to improve the upper registers. See Theobald Boehm, *The Flute and Flute-Playing*, trans. by Dayton C. Miller (NewYork: Dover Publications, Inc., 1964), pp. 19-20. (Facsimile of 1922 ed.)

some of the benefits conferred by the bell key without the necessity for drastic revision of their fingering technique.

The keyless recorder possesses sufficient resources for the satisfactory performance of the entire pre-twentieth century repertoire, and most of the contemporary repertoire as well, including the bulk of "avant-garde" literature. Its fingering system is relatively straightforward, though still far from simple. Since its fingerings require a minimum amount of intonation correction, it is easier than the bell-keyed recorder to play in tune. Its complete lack of keywork simplifies the problem of maintenance. The theoretical superiority of its low register has already been noted. The lack of a bell key does not exclude the possibility of closing the bell with the knee (a technique much used by the Dutch recorderists), and thus enjoying, to a limited extent, some of the faculties of the compromise recorder. The keyless recorder has, and always will have, musicological significance, as the authentic instrument of the baroque repertoire, particularly since certain recorder makers have begun to build replicas, or near-replicas, of some eighteenth-century recorders. A knowledge of its technique remains essential, since the piccolo recorders —the sixth flute (soprano in D), soprano, and sopranino—will probably continue to be built as keyless instruments only. Because of the quicker response and specialized nature of these smaller sizes of recorder, their keyless design remains quite adequate, particularly in the case of the sopranino. However, because of its restricted versatility, in comparison with the other two types of concert recorder, I regard the keyless concert recorder as an instrument of historical interest only. This is not meant in any way to disparage those recorderists who have accomplished, and will continue to accomplish, breathtaking feats of musicianship and technique on the keyless recorder.

CHAPTER II

Holding the Recorder

SUPPORTING THE INSTRUMENT

It is customary to speak of "holding the recorder." However, a more accurate expression would be "balancing the recorder." The former term implies that the recorder is to be "grasped." Nothing could be further from the truth. A firm grasp on the recorder precludes the attainment of good execution, which requires that the recorder be free to move and that the hands be as relaxed as possible. Both of these conditions become impossible to satisfy if the player tries to "hold" the recorder.

The recorder is, in fact, loosely *supported* or *balanced,* rather than rigidly *held.* It lies in a state of flexible, but secure, equilibrium. It should be possible to remove a correctly-supported recorder from the player's hands without the least hint of resistance. The achievement of such a state demands, in accordance with the laws of physics, that the instrument be supported at a minimum of three points. These points are provided by the right thumb, the lower lip, and one or more fingers, almost invariably those of the left hand.

The recorder rests principally on the right thumb. A thumbrest is indispensable to assure the requisite stability. It should be attached with glue or tape at a point somewhat to the left of the recorder's vertical axis (as viewed from the player's side), and opposite the space bounded vertically by the fifth and sixth holes. (The exact point of attachment can only be determined by the individual player.) One should never screw the thumbrest onto the recorder. The angle formed by the thumbrest and the tube of the recorder rests against the right thumb. The right edge of the thumb, adjacent to the quick, exerts pressure on the thumbrest, while the right half of the ball or fleshy pad of the thumb presses against the tube of the recorder. The thumbrest should be either made of cork or cork-bushed. The tube of the recorder should be covered with a thin sheet of cork at the point where it comes in contact with the thumb. The thumb should be negatively curved (i.e., curved backward) and held so that it forms an arc concentric with those made by the positively curved index- and middle-fingers of the right hand. The point of support provided by the right thumb constitutes the only stationary point along the entire length of the recorder during use. As such, it serves as the fulcrum on which the instrument pivots during breathing, and also, to a slight extent, during fingering.

The lower lip furnishes the second point of support. The tip of the concave lower surface of the mouthpiece rests on the lower lip while the instrument is in use. The upper lip provides additional stability by resting on the tip of the mouthpiece's convex upper surface, thus steadying the instrument. The mouthpiece must be kept dry. This may be assured by allowing it to come in contact only with the red portion of the lips. Under no circumstances should the player curl the lips over the teeth, clarinet-fashion, or worse, allow the teeth to touch the mouthpiece. Both lips must always be perfectly relaxed—one should guard against pursing or tensing them as if playing on a transverse flute. While sounding the recorder, both lips ordinarily remain in contact with the mouthpiece, and with each other. It makes no difference whether the mouthpiece lies at the exact center of the lips or a little to the side. When the player takes breath, the lower jaw and the mouthpiece drop, allowing air to enter through the space bounded by the upper surface of the mouthpiece and the lower lip on the one hand, and by the upper lip on the other. The mouthpiece *must* remain in contact with the lower lip during breathing. The taking of a breath thus involves the actual movement of the recorder. As has been stated above, the right thumb provides a fulcrum for this movement.

The third point of support is provided by one or more of the fingers, usually those of the left hand. The recorder is so constructed that all but two fingerings involve the closing of one or more left-hand finger-holes other than the thumbhole. (The left thumb is not considered to be a finger for the purposes of the present discussion. Since it lies on the same side of the recorder as the lower lip and the right-hand thumb, it is clearly unfit to render support under normal circumstances.) These two fingerings are alternate f#″ (1) and alternate g#″ (0), used for the whole-tone trills on e″ and f#″, respectively. Should additional support be required in these cases, it may be obtained by placing the right-hand little finger on its hole, or on the key. (One or more of the other right-hand fingers may be added, or substituted, for purposes of convenience or timbric alteration.) Otherwise, the placement of a finger on a hole, or worse, on the wood between holes, for purposes of support—the so-called "buttress-finger" technique—has no valid place in recorder technique. There are but three exceptions to this rule. When one removes the right hand from the recorder, in order to shade or cover the window, it is permissible to place the left-hand little finger on, or even behind, the recorder for additional support. When turning a page with the right hand while fingering f#″ or g″ in the usual fashion, one must support the instrument by placing the left-hand little finger on the wood, the first phalanx (i.e., the uppermost

joint) of the left-hand index finger against the ivory ring[1] or
torus at the base of the headpiece, and the left thumb on the
wood below the thumbhole, in lieu of the right thumb. Lastly,
if one were to turn a page while fingering f#″ with the thumb
alone, it would be necessary to place one or more of the left-
hand fingers on the wood to keep the instrument from falling.

THE POSITION OF THE HANDS

The classical hand-position in recorder-playing was described and illustrated as early as 1707 by Hotteterre-le Ro-
maine.[2] With certain important exceptions, most of Hotteterre's remarks on hand-position remain valid—particularly
his warning against constraint.[3]

The head and torso should be held upright and relaxed,
regardless of whether one stands or sits while playing. It is
better to stand, for this increases the capacity of the lungs,
facilitates the production of a full, controlled tone, promotes
the requisite alertness and concentration, and favors the projection of the recorder's sound to the audience. The music
stand should be set as low as possible with the desk tilted at
about forty-five degrees, to prevent its getting between the
audience and the instrument, thus muffling the tone and cre-
ating a visual barrier between audience and player. Lowering
the stand in this fashion also facilitates tone projection by
forcing the player to stoop slightly, thus holding the recorder
in an almost vertical position and pointing the window and
the fingerholes (from both of which most of the sound ema-
nates) more in the direction of the audience. The recorder
should be held so that the footpiece slants somewhat to the
player's right, for the convenience of the right hand. The arms

---

[1] On some recorders this is made of wood.

[2] Hotteterre, p. 73.

[3] *Ibid.*, p. 35.

should hang comfortably near the body. When playing standing up, one may either rest the weight of the body equally on both feet, or on the right foot, with the left foot forward and the left knee slightly bent, as in the classic flute-playing position.[4] It is best not to move the feet about while playing. Above all, the hands, arms, and the entire body should be relaxed and at ease.

The position of the right hand may show considerable variation from one player to another, depending on such factors as the length of the fingers in relation to that of the thumb. Those with relatively long fingers may find it advantageous to curve the fingers to a greater degree than those with shorter fingers. The important thing is that the action of the fingers be free. To insure this, one must see to it that the weight of the recorder is confined to the right thumb and the adjacent portion of the wrist and forearm (i.e., the base of the radius), rather than being placed across the knuckles of the remaining right-hand digits. It is useful to think of this weight as a stream or current, which must under no circumstances be allowed to intersect with the pathways formed by the muscles, tendons, and nerves that lead to, and control, the fingers other than the thumb. The fingers may be arched or straight, but never negatively curved, like the thumbs. They should rest *lightly* upon their holes, so that little or no imprint of the holes appears on their pads. The areas most suitable for use in stopping the holes vary from one finger to the next, and from one player to another. They generally tend to lie more on the soft fleshy pads than on the harder tips. The right wrist should be bent more or less inward, as on the transverse flute. The right-hand index finger should lean somewhat to the side, in the direction of the mouthpiece. The right-hand little finger will usually lie almost straight.

The position of the left hand is more crucial than that of the right. On it depends the control of the speaker-vents, and

[4] For a description of this position, see Rockstro, p. 419.

hence, register selection, intonation control, dynamic variation, and tonal nuance. Consequently, the left-hand position
tends to exhibit a greater degree of uniformity than that of
the right hand, among players who appreciate the necessity
for such control.

In order to attain proper control of the speaker-vents,
one must abandon the classical left-hand position, as described
and illustrated in Hotteterre's *Treatise on the Recorder*,[5] sub-
stituting in its stead a somewhat modified version of the left-
hand position associated with the transverse flute. In this position, the left wrist is turned somewhat clockwise, and bent
inward almost as far as it will go, so that the first and second
phalanges or joints of the left index finger either touch the
wood or ivory ring at the juncture of the head- and center-
pieces, or else come very close to doing so. The first phalanx
or uppermost joint is elevated so that it forms an angle with
the metacarpal bone. This phalanx will then point almost directly forward and to the front of the player, rather than off
to the side, as in the classical position. The index and middle
fingers of the left hand should be curved considerably more
than the left ring finger, which lies almost straight, like the
little finger of the right hand. The left-hand thumb is negatively curved, except when pinching.[6] It either touches, or
lies very close to, the base or metacarpal bone of the index
finger. It also lies nearly parallel to the base of the index finger. This position of the left thumb represents a departure
from that assumed by this digit on the Boehm transverse
flute. (However, on the baroque one-keyed flute, the thumb
may be held as described above.) A less apparent but equally
important difference between left-hand position on recorder
and transverse flute is that all digits, *including* the left index

[5] Hotteterre, pp. 72-73.
[6] When executing passages in which pinched notes alternate with those in which
the thumbhole is completely open, the thumb remains in this positively curved
pinching position.

finger, normally move from the knuckles on the recorder. (On the flute, the second and third phalanges of the index finger move independently, while the first phalanx remains stationary to provide support for the instrument.)

The left-hand position advocated above assigns the task of controlling the size of the critical uppermost thumbhole aperture formed in pinching to a stronger, more centralized portion of the thumbnail than the classical left-hand position, which gives this formidable duty to the weak left-hand edge of the thumbnail, the irregularly-shaped cuticle, and the soft, fleshy part of the thumb. In addition to these weaknesses, the classical left-hand position makes half-holing and second-position pinching more difficult. For these reasons, adherence to the classical position makes it virtually impossible to play into the high registers with full control and assurance. It also places obstacles in the way of intonation control and dynamic and tonal inflection. Before the appearance of the bell-keyed recorder, when the recorder was considered a doubler's instrument and expected to confine itself to a melodic range of less than two octaves, such limitations were of little importance. Today it has become absolutely essential to maximize control over all facets of recorder technique, on bell-keyed and keyless instruments alike. The old hand position has outlived its usefulness; it should be abandoned.

The need for maximum relaxation and freedom from constraint in holding the recorder and positioning the hands and body must again be emphasized. Any stiffness in the knuckles or fingers, or in the left wrist is a sign of undue tension. However, some stiffness at the base of the right thumb after a long playing session may occur in spite of all precautions to minimize tension. This is normal, and should be a signal for the player to take a rest.

CHAPTER III

Tonguing

The tongue serves three functions in recorder technique. It controls the duration of the notes by acting as their initiator and terminator. It plays a major role in register selection; i.e., in determining which of several possible modes or registers will sound with a given fingering. Lastly, it plays a role in enabling the player to emphasize or de-emphasize different notes through variation in the strength of the attack. The use of the tongue in recorder-playing is called "tonguing."

There are three normal types of tonguing: single-tonguing, staccato-tonguing, and double-tonguing. No sharp dividing line exists between the first two. All three make use of two basic tongue-strokes and variations derived therefrom: the attack-stroke and the preparatory or silent stroke. The attack-stroke occurs when the upper surface of the tongue, near the tip, moves forward and downward, from a position of rest against the palate, so that it plucks or brushes against the dental ridge of the palate. This stroke is often likened to the whispered syllable "tah"; however, "dah" represents a somewhat closer approximation of the actual tongue-stroke. The strength of the tongue-stroke is a function of the velocity of the tongue and the distance which it travels; these in turn vary directly with the degree of pressure exerted by the tongue against the palate in plucking, and the distance from the teeth of the point of contact with the tongue. It is one of the variables governing register selection. In general, it increases as one ascends towards the higher registers and decreases as one descends towards the bottom notes of the instrument. For the lowest tones, the tongue-stroke may approximate a softly-whispered "nah," rather than the more usual "dah." This relationship between the strength of the tongue-stroke and the pitch of the note is subject to some exceptions. For example, when taken with the traditional keyless fingerings, $c\sharp'''$ and f''' are tongued gently, as if they were low notes, rather than middle-range notes. To understand the reason for these variations in the strength of the tongue-stroke, one must understand that each note (or, more accurately, each fingering-mode combination) must be attacked with a certain carefully-controlled initial pulse of air. This pulse of air is impelled and controlled by the attack-stroke of the tongue. Furthermore, the amount of air necessary to initiate a tone differs radically, in most cases, from the amount of air necessary to sustain it. Hence the attack must be controlled independently of, and treated quite differently from, the sustained portion of the note. The low notes require a very gentle, gradually increasing pulse of air for their initiation, and consequently, a very gentle attack-stroke. They require considerably more air to sustain them than to attack them. Hence, the strength of the airstream increases after the attack. The higher notes, in contrast, require a relatively strong, abrupt pulse of air for their initiation, and consequently, a stronger, sharper attack-stroke than the lower notes. They require considerably less air to sustain them than to attack them. Thus, the strength of the airstream decreases after the attack. A graphic representation of the relative amounts of air needed for the attacks and the sustained portions of low tones and high tones, along with the rate at which the air pressure changes during the attack, would look something like this:

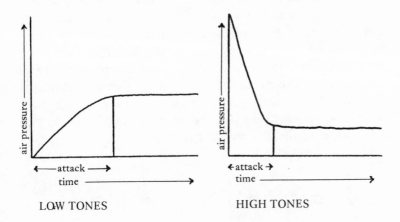

LOW TONES   HIGH TONES

Further discussion of the airstream must be deferred until the next chapter. For the present, it is sufficient to observe that while one *tongues* more forcefully as one goes up the scale, one *blows* relatively more gently as one ascends. This is the opposite of what most players have believed, from Hotteterre's day to the present. The traditional view resulted from a failure to distinguish between the attack and the sustained portion of the note. Failure to regulate the strength of the tongue-stroke according to these principles results in the production of momentary impurities, known as "chiff," at the instant that the note begins to sound.

As one ascends, the vowel sounds of the attack-stroke change from "ah" to "ee." High notes, then, are attacked with the syllable "dee." This change, which occurs in both staccato-tonguing and double-tonguing, as well as in single-tonguing, relates, properly speaking, to the embouchure, rather than the tongue-stroke; however, its intimate association with the latter necessitates some mention of it in this chapter. A fuller discussion of this phenomenon and the reasons behind it appears in the following chapter.

Once the tongue has executed its attack-stroke, it must move backward and upward, so that it touches the palate, in order to prepare to deliver the next attack-stroke. This movement, which should be delayed in direct proportion to the degree of legato that one wishes to produce, in order that it may occur as closely as desired to the beginning of the next note, constitutes the preparatory stroke or silent stroke. Both it and the attack-stroke may be approximated by whispering "dah, uh-dah, uh-dah," in this rhythm:

It is worth noting that the preparatory stroke takes place while the note immediately preceding the one to be attacked is still sounding—in other words, *before* the fingers have changed position for the next note. Failure to appreciate this fact is largely responsible for the difficulties experienced by beginning and intermediate students in synchronizing the fingers with the tongue.

In legato-tonguing, the preparatory stroke should interrupt the airstream for as short a time as possible. In normal staccato-tonguing, the preparatory stroke is transformed into a stroke of termination, by allowing the tongue to remain in contact with the palate and postponing the attack-stroke that would normally follow immediately after the preparatory stroke, as if whispering "dit, dit, dit." To understand this stroke of termination, one has only to imagine the manner in which many Americans pronounce their final "t"s. The word "it," for example, is often pronounced not "i-tuh," but "i(t)," with a silent "t," in which the tongue, after terminating the airstream, remains in contact with the palate, like the

tangent of a clavichord, as opposed to the hammer of a pi-
anoforte.

There are two additional methods of staccato-tonguing, the
first useful for obtaining moderate separation between notes,
the second interchangeable with normal staccato-tonguing. In
the first of these, one terminates the notes with the diaphragm (i.e., with the breath alone), rather than with the
tongue, so that the preparatory stroke occurs between tones:

Larghetto

Da - da - da - da - da - da - da - da - da.

This method of articulation, while employed extensively on
the transverse flute, can only be used effectively in the low
register on the recorder. If used above the low register, an
unwanted lower tone would be heard momentarily at the end
of each note, because the diaphragm cannot terminate the
airstream as suddenly as the tongue, and the relatively gradual
drop in the strength of the airstream would cause a lower register tone to sound.

The second additional method of staccato-tonguing should
really be called slow double-tonguing, since it is identical in
all respects except speed to my preferred method of double-
tonguing, as described below. With this method, one may
either terminate the notes with the tongue or, in the low register, with the diaphragm.

Since it is physically impossible to single-tongue passages
with more than about 320 notes per minute or more than
four notes per beat at a metronome setting of about 80, such
passages must be double-tongued. In double-tonguing, the
preparatory stroke becomes a second attack-stroke, in which
some part of the tongue other than that used for single-tonguing brushes against the palate. In executing this second attack-
stroke, the tongue reverses direction, moving backward and

upward, rather than forward and downward. The tongue becomes, in effect, a rocker or seesaw, with the fulcrum lying
between the tip and that part of the tongue which alternates
with the tip in delivering the attack-stroke. The type of double-tonguing is determined by the part of the tongue which
one uses for the second attack-stroke. There are three possible
varieties of double-tonguing on the recorder. Of these, one is
almost useless, one has only limited application, and the third
may be considered ideally suited for use in recorder-playing.

The most commonly used method of double-tonguing on
most present-day wind instruments involves the alternation
of the normal attack-stroke with a special attack-stroke produced by brushing the rear portion of the tongue's upper surface against the back of the palate, as when whispering the
syllable "guh." This type of double-tonguing consists of a
succession of the syllables "di-guh, di-guh." The syllable
"di" (pronounced with a short *i* as in the word *bit*) must
always fall on the strong beat. For triplets, many players employ the so-called triple-tonguing, consisting of the syllables
"di-guh-di, di-guh-di." However, these types of rapid articulation have several disadvantages, which disqualify them for
general use on the recorder, in my opinion.[1] The radical
dissimilarity between the two attack-strokes involved makes a
natural, automatic transition between single- and double-
tonguing more difficult to achieve. The "guh" attack-stroke
is manifestly unsuited for control of register selection, particularly in the recorder's upper range. It cannot deliver a carefully controlled pulse of air with the ease and precision of the
normal attack-stroke. Furthermore, the difficulty of articu-
lating two "guh" strokes in succession forces the player to
adopt a mechanical approach towards double-tonguing, by

---

[1] It must be admitted, however, that this form of double-tonguing *can* be developed to a high degree of perfection. Indeed, some players find themselves physically incapable of mastering any other type but this. In such cases, there are, of
course, no objections to its use. See below, p. 33.

forcing him to determine in advance which syllables to use for each note in rapid passages. It thus makes a conscious act out of something which should occur automatically. This places an additional burden on the player. Finally, this method of double-tonguing exerts a harmful influence on recorder embouchure, and hence, on tone quality. Nevertheless, it does have some limited uses. One or more pairs of short notes occurring among longer ones in moderately fast pieces may, if desired, be double-tongued in this fashion to achieve a crisp, marcato effect—provided that the passage in question lies in the low or lower-middle registers.

Dah di-guh dah di-guh dit   dit   di-guh dah dah(t).

This form of double-tonguing may also be used for slow passages, at least in theory, for a staccato or moderately legato effect, or anything in between. Its use here would, however, be unnecessary, from a practical point of view, since these effects may be produced more easily by other means.

A second variety of double-tonguing, and one advocated by Quantz and others,[2] is produced by alternating the normal attack-stroke with one obtained by brushing the edge of the mid-portion of the tongue against the palate, at a point somewhere between the dental ridge and the area used for the syllable "guh." It can best be performed by whispering the syllables "di-d'll, di-d'll," taking care to pronounce the second syllable crisply, with rigid tongue, in the German manner. With all due respect to the woodwind players of the past who advocated this method of double-tonguing, I cannot recommend its use on the recorder, except possibly for a short string of

[2] Quantz, pp. 79-84; Anthony Baines, *Woodwind Instruments and their History* (3rd ed., London: Faber and Faber Ltd., 1967), p. 42.

rapidly repeated notes in the low or lower-middle registers, when a special legato effect is desired:

Presto   ($\quad$ = ca. 168)

Di - d'll,   di - d'll,   di - d'll,   di - d'll   dah(t).

Besides being every bit as mechanical as "di-guh, di-guh," it lacks definition and interferes with the embouchure even more. The "d'll" stroke causes the tongue to impede the free flow of air into the instrument. It seems virtually impossible to synchronize this type of double-tonguing with the fingers. Not even its most enthusiastic present-day advocates have been successful in doing so, to my knowledge.

The third and most useful variety of double-tonguing consists of the alternation of the standard attack-stroke with a second attack-stroke derived from the preparatory stroke of ordinary single-tonguing, and produced by brushing the upper surface of the tongue immediately behind the portion used for the normal attack-stroke against the dental ridge of the palate, as when whispering the syllables "di-duh, di-duh" (or "di-ri, di-ri," in German[3]). This was a standard method of double-tonguing before 1820, when it was superseded by "di-guh, di-guh."[4] Because of the similarity between the two tongue-strokes involved, because the same portion of the palate is used for both, and because the second attack-stroke derives directly from the ordinary .silent stroke, this form of double-tonguing, once mastered, is virtually free from all the objections that have been raised against the other two. It permits the player to mix the two attack-strokes with great freedom, since both are identical in practice, though not in

[3] See Quantz, pp. 76-79.
[4] Baines, pp. 42-44.

theory. (Indeed, the player is usually unconscious of the distinction between the two.) It detracts only slightly from tone quality and ease of register selection. It demands no premeditation from the player. It permits an absolutely smooth transition between single- and double-tonguing. It even removes the need to regard triple-tonguing as a separate technical problem. In short, it represents the perfect solution to virtually all articulation problems requiring double-tonguing on the recorder.

Its mastery may occasion some initial difficulties for the player. Indeed, some persons appear to be physically incapable of executing it (see above, p. 30, n. 1). (Such individuals have no alternative but to make adopt "di-guh, di-guh" as their normal form of double-tonguing.) If the player whispers the words "to do, to do" over and over again, at an increasing rate of speed, he will soon learn to execute this form of double-tonguing[5] —provided, of course, that he is physically able to do so. Anthony Baines relates that the flutist Drouet "used to teach [it to] his English pupils by means of the word 'territory'," as pronounced by the British, with the dental "R."[6] It is difficult for the beginner to practice it in slow motion for purposes of study. When practiced slowly, it is transformed into the second of the two additional varieties of staccato-tonguing mentioned above (see p. 29).

Some musicians have argued that this method of double-tonguing is not double-tonguing at all.[7] However, since the two attack-strokes involve movements in opposite directions, as well as two slightly different areas of the tongue, if not of the palate, this argument is manifestly untenable.[8]

The easiest way to master this form of double-tonguing is simply to practice it. Detailed analysis of the order of the

[5] See Rockstro, p. 509.
[6] Baines, p. 42.
[7] See, for example, Rockstro, p. 509.
[8] *Ibid.*

two attack-strokes has little practical value, besides being
fraught with difficulties. However, for the sake of theoretical
comprehensiveness, some observations on the theoretical ar-
rangement of the tongue-strokes are given below.

Analysis of the two strokes seems to indicate that the normal attack-stroke—nominally the stronger of the two—tends
to fall on downbeats or odd-numbered notes, while the secondary attack-stroke usually occurs on upbeats or even-
numbered notes. However, this does not imply any inevitable
inequality in accentuation, nor does it entail any rhythmic inequality of the sort exemplified by the French *inégal*. It does
not result from any conscious effort on the player's part.

Triplet figures may be tongued using simple alternation
of the two attack-strokes. However, when one wishes to accent the first note of each triplet, the following pattern sometimes results:

This may, for the sake of theoretical comprehensiveness, be
classified as triple-tonguing. However, the fact remains that
the player is seldom conscious of the difference between, or
the order of, the two attack-strokes. The player should strive
to make the two attack-strokes as equal as possible, so that
they may be employed interchangeably when necessary. In
practice, the necessity for such employment arises constantly.
The resulting theoretical complexities seem to defy rational
analysis.

All double-tongued passages are, by definition, performed
more or less staccato. The degree of staccato may be varied
to some extent, by controlling the duration of the individual
notes, within narrow limits. Normally, the player should strive
to make his double-tongued passages sound as legato as pos-

sible. However, passages involving many awkward finger movements in succession should be played as staccatissimo as possible, in order to conceal the inevitable minor inaccuracies in fingering. The shorter the notes, the more time the fingers have to execute their movements unheard, in the intervals between tones. But this expedient should not be abused; a quick tongue is no substitute for brilliant fingers. Most recorderists tend to overlook the legato possibilities of the recorder, choosing to chirp rather than sing on their instrument. Slurring is every bit as effective on the recorder as on the other woodwinds. The execution of even lengthy passages without the use of the tongue constitutes one of the beauties of the recorder.

Generally speaking, slow movements should be played more legato than fast ones, depending, of course, on the particular emotional content of the passages in question. One should almost always take care to make some separation between repeated notes, lest they sound like one long, unbroken tone.

It should be noted that the vowel sounds in double-tonguing vary according to the register in which one plays, though to a lesser extent than in single-tonguing. Since the attack occupies a far greater proportion of the note in double-tonguing than in single-tonguing, these variations lose much of their importance. They influence the sustained portion of the note, rather than the initial portion, during which the attack occurs.

To accent a note, one increases the strength of the air-stream with the diaphragm. In the higher registers, one may also increase the strength of the tongue-stroke. In the lowest part of the range, any attempt to do so may result in overblowing, unless this tendency is counteracted by the embouchure. Thus, the role of the tongue in emphasis is subsidiary to its other functions, though far from insignificant.

Although recorder technique is vastly more complicated than is generally believed, tonguing is considerably more

straightforward a subject than most musicians realize. Unlike
other aspects of recorder technique, it takes care of itself,
once the basic principles have been mastered. I therefore consider it unnecessary to distinguish among a large variety of
articulation syllables, as do Ganassi[9] and others, or to pursue
the subject much further. Those who master the basic principles of tonguing will easily know how to produce all the
subtleties of articulation, without recourse to a mechanical
assortment of special tonguing syllables.

Mention should, however, be made of the so-called "as-
pirated attack," described by Michael Vetter.[10] This consists
of the attack of the note with the diaphragm, rather than the
tongue. To execute it, one whispers "ha." It is occasionally
useful in the lower registers when a soft attack is desired. It
is impractical in the higher registers. It finds its most important application, however, in conjunction with what I shall
call the "finger attack," to assure the precise and immediate
articulation of initial low-register tones at full strength on the
larger, slower-speaking sizes of recorder (such as the notes
below $a^{b'}$ on the tenor). In performing the finger attack
(which, by the way, is borrowed from Boehm flute technique),
the player taps one or more fingers down onto the holes with
sufficient force to pressurize the air column, at the exact
point in time at which one wishes the note to speak. Fingers
3 and 4 should usually be used on the recorder. This technique may also be used in conjunction with the conventional
tongue-stroke.

The so-called "lip attack"[11] has no place in traditionally-
oriented recorder technique.

‣ There exists the possibility of deliberately using the clicks
caused by slurring across register breaks to produce a type of

---

[9] Sylvestro Ganassi, *Opera Intitulata Fontegara,* ed. and trans. by Hildemarie
   Peter; English translation from the 1956 German ed. by Dorothy Swainson (Ber-
   lin-Lichterfelde: Robert Lienau, 1959), pp. 12, 14.
[10] Michael Vetter, *Il Flauto Dolce et Acerbo* (Celle: Moeck Verlag, 1969), p. 58.
[11] *Ibid.*

articulation. This, however, concerns fingering, rather than tonguing. The type of articulation one wishes to produce constitutes one of the factors governing selection of fingerings.

A tone is normally terminated either by the preparatory tongue-stroke for the succeeding tone, by a stroke of termination[12] (the usual way of ending the final note of a piece), or by the sudden reversal of the airstream—i.e., by taking a breath. One writer advocates the removal of the mouthpiece from the lips as a means of terminating the final note of a piece.[13] Although there is nothing to be said against this practice, it seems easier to make use of the tongue. One should guard against ending a tone with a gradual decrease of the airstream, unassisted by the tongue, as on the transverse flute, except to achieve a glissando, as a special effect. (The production of a diminuendo is another matter; but here the tongue still effects the termination of the note.) This seemingly obvious precaution is frequently ignored.

Although a discussion of the movements of the jaw in recorder-playing belongs, in theory, in the section on embouchure in the following chapter, the close association of these movements with those of the tongue makes it necessary to deal with them here. For the tone to be round and pure, the oral cavity must be open. This is accomplished by opening the jaw about halfway, while keeping the lips in contact with the mouthpiece and with each other. However, the tongue, being attached to the lower jaw, cannot possibly reach up to the palate to initiate the attack or the termination from this position. Hence the necessity for closing the jaw almost completely during the preparatory stroke and dropping it during the attack-stroke, when single-tonguing. These motions will occur more or less naturally if one stands before a mirror and whispers the syllables of single-tonguing: "Dah, uh-dah, uh-dah—(t)." (This is the reason why a good recorderist seems

---

[12] See above, p. 28.

[13] A. Rowland-Jones, *Recorder Technique* (London: Oxford University Press, 1959), p. 65.

to be "chewing" on his notes in passages of slow and moderate tempi.) Needless to say, the jaw must be kept loose and relaxed. During these movements, the mouthpiece will move up and down with the lower jaw, causing the recorder to pivot on the right thumb, as described in the previous chapter.

These movements of the jaw occur only in slow and moderate single- and staccato-tonguing. In double-tonguing and in fast single-tonguing, the jaw remains in an almost closed position, with the front teeth about one-quarter of an inch apart.

To conclude this chapter, the reader should again be warned (as he already has been in the Preface to this book) against the distortions that must inevitably arise when one attempts to codify in writing what is essentially a nonverbal art. Thus, although the foregoing discussion of the use of the tongue in recorder-playing may seem mechanical and artificial, one must nevertheless try to perceive the actual process as something dynamic, natural, and free from the fetters of pedantic rules. Such rules emerge *after* the fact, not before it, when one attempts to describe a process which refuses to be bound by the limitations of verbal expression.

CHAPTER IV

Tone

EMBOUCHURE

On most woodwinds, embouchure consists of the shaping of the lips and tongue to control the tone. In recorder technique, the definition of embouchure must be expanded to include the shaping of any and all parts of the respiratory tract to control the tone. For although the lips play only a minor role in recorder embouchure (and this only in the production of special effects[1]), the throat, sinus cavities, tongue, and diaphragm assume many of the functions normally performed by the lips on the other major woodwinds. Still other duties performed by the embouchure on these other woodwinds are given to the speaker-vents, as will be seen in the next chapter. Hence the role of the embouchure on the recorder, where one must work within the limitations of a fixed windway, appears rather restricted in comparison with the other wind instruments. Indeed, one can play the recorder fairly well with little or no knowledge of recorder embouchure. However, without this knowledge, one will never be

---

[1] See Vetter, p. 55.

able to reveal the true beauties of the instrument. The mastery of embouchure is therefore every bit as vital for the serious recorderist as it is for those who wish to achieve excellence on the flute, oboe, clarinet, or bassoon.

The Supporting Function of the Diaphragm

Since the recorder offers less resistance to the player's breath than the other woodwinds, some means must be found to provide the steadiness and support that is furnished by the lips or the reed on these other instruments. The most satisfactory method for achieving this consists of the use of the diaphragm. The diaphragm provides the basis for, and control of, the airstream. All tones, whatever their register, originate ultimately from the diaphragm. This muscle controls the strength of the airstream, and thus plays an important role in dynamic variation, accent, and, particularly in the highest registers, register selection. One should always feel that the tone is supported by a jet of air, originating from the diaphragm and traveling through a bull's-eye, represented by the recorder's windway.

In the previous chapter, it was stated that "one blows relatively more gently as one ascends," in contradistinction to the generally held belief. The word "relatively" must be emphasized in the above sentence, lest the reader get the wrong impression. It is probably true that the amount of air needed to sustain the tone increases as one ascends. Nevertheless, it increases at a much smaller rate than does the maximum amount of air that the tone will bear without cracking or going sharp. Moreover, the *optimum* strength of air, relative to the range of air pressure over which the note will continue to sound, does decrease as one goes higher. For example, if low a′ requires seven-eighths of the maximum pressure of air that it can bear in order to sound with a good strong tone, and thus to match the naturally more vigorous tones of the higher registers, then g‴ may require no more than one-eighth the amount of air that it can stand, if it is to sound with a sweet, gentle tone, and thus to match the naturally weaker lower tones. Such adjustments in the strength of the airstream may be compared, in principle, to the graduated income tax. One gives the weak tones "financial assistance" in the form of as much air as they will bear, in order to strengthen them. At the same time, one "taxes" the naturally overassertive high tones by taking increasingly more air away from them, as one goes up the scale. (The middle tones take care of themselves.) The effect of these adjustments is to produce a musical, homogeneous effect from the inherently disparate registers of the recorder. Hence, the assertion that one blows less strongly as one ascends has musical, psychological, and pedagogical validity, even if it cannot bear scrutiny as a statement of scientific fact.[2]

In order to sustain the notes of the different registers according to these principles (rather than by simply varying the strength of the airstream in direct proportion to the pitch of the note, as is usually done), the player must make use of other embouchure techniques, which shall now be examined. It should be noted, however, that the system of control described here begins to break down when one ascends above b‴. The highest tones, such as d‴′, are obtained largely through lung power alone. One simply increases the strength of the airstream by means of the diaphragm until they sound.

The Placement of the Airstream

Although all tones have the diaphragm as their primary point of origin, they have a secondary point of origin as well. The diaphragm merely provides the requisite support or pressure for a fine tone; the actual tone may originate elsewhere, along a continuum or gradient extending from the bottom of the chest, through the throat, to the sinus cavities of the

[2] *Cf.* Quantz, pp. 54-55, 110.

head, depending on the frequency or pitch. The lowest tones (f'-g'') originate at the bottom of the chest, at the diaphragm. The lower middle tones (g''-c''') originate from the mid-portion of the chest (even though they are still supported by pressure from the diaphragm). The upper-middle tones (c'''-g''') stem from the throat. The highest tones (above g''') stem from the sinus cavities or head resonators. They, like the upper-middle tones, still retain the support of the diaphragm.

It will be seen that the foregoing techniques correspond closely to those used by singers. This correspondence is no accident. It is equally striking when one considers the role of the throat in recorder embouchure.

The Use of the Throat in Recorder Embouchure

The actions of the throat in recorder embouchure were accurately, albeit unwittingly, described by Quantz more than two hundred years ago:

> A low note results when you expand the opening of the windpipe by means of the appropriate muscles, and thus depress the five cartilages of which the larynx consists so that the said larynx is shortened slightly while you simultaneously exhale the air rather slowly from the lungs; the depth of this note depends upon the degree of expansion of the opening of the windpipe. A higher note results when you contract the opening of the windpipe, with the aid of the other muscles appointed for this purpose, and in consequence the aforementioned five cartilages in the larynx rise, making the windpipe somewhat narrower and longer, while you simultaneously exhale the air from the lungs more rapidly; the height of this note depends upon the narrowness of the opening.[3]

---

[3] Quantz, p. 49. Quoted by permission of the publishers, Faber and Faber, London, and the Macmillan Publishing Co., Inc., New York. Copyright © Faber and Faber 1966.

In recorder-playing, the throat undergoes the same changes when passing from one register to another as it does in singing. In both cases, it relaxes for the lowest tones and gradually tightens as one ascends, thus constricting the airstream in direct proportion to the rise in pitch. By constricting the airstream, the throat serves the same function in recorder-playing as do the lips in flute-playing: it causes the air to flow faster, and thus to excite the higher modes or registers of the air column. Thus, the throat represents an important factor in register selection. The use of the throat to increase the speed of the airstream obviates, or at least greatly reduces, the necessity of simply blowing harder—and more loudly—as one goes up the scale. It thus facilitates the maintenance of a more homogeneous dynamic level over the entire melodic range of the instrument. Hence, proper control of the throat is absolutely essential to the production of a fine tone, particularly on the bell-keyed recorder, with its extended upper range.

Such control of the throat is not as hard to achieve as it may seem. The player has only to imagine that he is singing the note he wishes to play, while at the same time blowing the high notes as softly as possible without cracking them. The throat will automatically make the necessary adjustments. Its movements may be observed, to some extent, by standing in front of a mirror. In the high registers, the Adam's apple rises; in the low registers it drops. This is most apparent when executing slurred octaves above c''.

The throat also plays a role in the attack, and in minimizing the clicks that occur when slurring across register breaks, as well as in subduing similar impurities that occur when executing difficult finger changes in slurred passages. At such instants, careful observation before a mirror reveals that the Adam's apple drops momentarily, as when grunting, particularly when slurring *downward* across a register break. In all probability, the throat, assisted by the diaphragm, momentarily interrupts the airstream, either completely or partially, thus eliminating unwanted noises between notes. It plays a secondary role (in conjunction with the tongue-stroke) in regulating the rate of increase of the airstream during the attack, and after the momentary interruptions of the tone described above. In addition, the constriction of the throat is greater at the moment of attack than during the sustained portion of the note, in the higher registers. The reverse holds true in the low register.

The louder one plays, the more open the throat should be. As one gets softer, the throat becomes more constricted. Here again, the similarity between the recorderist's throat and the transverse flutist's lips is readily apparent. In this case, however, the change cannot be perceived when one stands before a mirror.

The Role of the Tongue, Oral Cavity, and Sinus Cavities in Recorder Embouchure

The tongue and oral cavity play a major role in recorder embouchure, by virtue of their ability to determine the formation of different vowel sounds, in conjunction with the sinus cavities. As was stated in the previous chapter, each part of the range must be sounded with a different vowel sound— "ah" for the low register, and "ee" for the higher registers. This change from low to high takes place gradually rather than abruptly, as one ascends. To explain it, one has recourse to the theory of formants, which states that each vowel sound has its own pitch.[4] By proper selection of vowel sounds, and also by silently "singing" the note being played, the recorderist shapes the oral cavity, the sinus cavities, and the entire respiratory system so that the entire respiratory system resonates with the note, and thus facilitates its production and control. The easiest way to grasp these techniques is, once

---

[4] A fuller discussion of the theory of formants may be found in Philip Bate, *The Oboe*, rev. ed. (London: Ernest Benn Ltd., 1962), pp. 111-114.

again, to imagine that one is singing the note one wishes to obtain. The player should, in addition, experiment with different vowel sounds in order to develop an awareness of their effect on the tone. It should be remembered that the internal structure of the respiratory tract (particularly of the oral and sinus cavities) may vary as much from one player to the next as do the lips of different transverse flutists; consequently what works for one player may have to be modified for another.

When playing softly up around $b^{b'''}$ with the proper embouchure as described above, the player may experience a choking or gagging sensation. This is a normal result of the correct placement of the throat, oral cavity, sinus cavities, and airstream necessary for these notes.

In addition to its role in determining the vowel sound, the oral cavity serves as the recorder's wind chest (to borrow a term from organ technology). As such it must normally be as wide open as possible, except during the tongue-stroke, to allow free passage of air into the instrument. However, occasions arise when the player may wish to impede the airstream's passage by more or less closing the jaw. Such occasions present themselves when the player wishes to muffle the tone, and also when playing pianissimo. In addition, d'''' and other extremely high notes often tend to speak more easily when the jaw is almost closed.

The player may also control the tone by means of the cheek pockets. Normally, the cheeks should be kept firm and immobile, so that they do not move with the vibrato pulsations. They must always be kept this way in double-tongued passages, for the sake of clean execution. When one wishes to dampen or sweeten the tone somewhat, particularly in the higher registers, they may be relaxed and puffed out so that they move with the player's vibrato. When playing pianissimo, the cheeks should be completely relaxed and the jaw rather closed, so that the oral cavity may assist in preserving the steadiness of the tone, which otherwise tends to deteriorate at low dynamic levels. It should be noted that b′″ is normally played with the cheeks completely relaxed.

BREATHING AND BREATH CONTROL

Since the techniques of breathing in recorder-playing are identical to those used in transverse flute-playing, the student may wish to supplement the present discussion with readings from the excellent literature on transverse flute technique.[5]

For purposes of convenience, one may distinguish three kinds of breaths in recorder-playing: the full breath, the normal breath, and the quick breath. These distinctions are relative rather than absolute. In all three breaths, the player takes in air through the mouth (as described in Chapter II), never through the nose. During all three breaths, the throat should be as open as possible, as when yawning.

Before beginning to play—and before taking a full breath —the player must take anywhere from fifteen seconds to a minute or more to prepare the lungs (and indeed, the entire body) for the physical and mental exercise of recorder-playing. He first exhales slowly and naturally, usually through the mouth, unburdening the lungs of excess air and reducing them to a state of "comfortable exhaustion," in which the lungs, though relatively depleted of air and ready to take in a fresh supply, do not require air desperately. It is especially vital to rid the upper half of the lungs of as much vitiated air as possible. Failure to accomplish this interferes with good

[5] The following selections are especially recommended: Quantz, pp. 87-90; F.B. Chapman, *Flute Technique* (3rd ed., London: Oxford University Press, 1958), pp. 1-3; Hans-Peter Schmitz, *School of Flute-Playing* (Kassel: Bärenreiter, Vol. I, trans. by Evelyn Frank; Vol. II, trans. by John Hays; 1966), Vol. I, pp. 20-21, Vol. II, pp. 5-6; and Roger S. Stevens, *Artistic Flute Technique and Study*, ed. by Ruth N. Zwissler (Hollywood: Highland Music Company, 1967), pp. 18-21. The present discussion owes much to these works, as well as to the insights of my teachers, particularly Samuel Baron.

breath control and proper support of the tone, and may cause
the player to break down completely in the middle of a piece
for want of air. At the same time, the player collects his mental and emotional facilities. He turns his attention to the
tempo, character, and general technical aspects of the piece
to be played, and assumes a suitable frame of mind for the
realization of his intentions in these areas, which, collectively,
constitute his "interpretation." If performing in public, he
masters his nervousness and ascertains the readiness of his fel-
low musicians. Towards the end of this period of preparation,
the player takes his first breath—almost always a slow one,
whether it be a full breath or a normal breath.

The breath taken during the period of preparation—before
one begins to play—is generally a full breath, unless the music
consists mainly of short phrases, offering numerous opportunities for frequent replenishment of the air supply, or unless
the piece is being performed on one of the piccolo recorders,
which require less air than the concert recorder. In such cases,
one usually begins with a normal breath. The full breath may
also be taken during a long enough rest. It may take anywhere from five to thirty seconds to execute, depending on
its size and the state of exhaustion of the air supply. To execute it, one first fills the lower part of the respiratory tract
by means of the diaphragm, so that the stomach wall moves
outward. This being accomplished, one proceeds to fill the
upper part of the chest so that the shoulders rise and the rib
cage expands. If still more air is required, one "tops off"
the air supply by gulping air with the throat, as if gasping. In
expending this air, the procedure should be reversed. One
empties the throat first, then the upper part of the chest, so
that the shoulders fall and the rib cage contracts; finally the
lower part of the respiratory tract is emptied, so that the upper two-thirds of the stomach wall moves inward. The lowest
third of the stomach wall remains relatively stationary. It
constitutes the primary point of support for the airstream,
against which the player presses, in lieu of the reed of the

oboe or bassoon. This area is under the direct control of the
diaphragm, which acts as the principal propelling force and
valve of the airstream. The throat also functions as a valve to
provide secondary support for the airstream by constricting
in the upper registers and in pianissimo passages, and thus
maintaining a reduced flow of air at a steady pressure. (See
the preceding section on embouchure in this chapter.)

The importance of exhausting the air supply in the sequence outlined above must again be emphasized. Adherence
to this sequence, together with the maintenance of firm diaphragmatic support, and the requisite amount of constriction
of the throat, represents the key to proper breath control in
recorder-playing.

The normal breath and the quick breath both represent
incomplete versions of the full breath. The normal breath is
executed by filling only the lower part of the respiratory tract
with the diaphragm, so that the stomach wall moves outward.
Mastery of this technique may be considerably facilitated by
employment of an old woodwind exercise, in which one lies
down, places a book on the stomach, and breathes in and out
so that the book rises and falls. This is the most usual recorder
breath, particularly on the piccolo recorders. It should be
practiced as silently as possible. A noisy breath indicates constriction and insufficient relaxation of the throat. By opening
the throat more (as if yawning or whispering "hoo" while inhaling) and by taking every breath as slowly as possible within
its allotted space of time, however small this may be, breath
noise can generally be minimized. However, the ability to
take in a large amount of air within a short space of time is of
far greater importance than the audibility of the breath.

Sometimes circumstances permit only the shortest of
breaths. In such instances (as, for example, when one must
take in air during an uninterrupted passage of sixteenth-notes
in an allegro), the quick breath finds its application. To exe-

cute it, one gulps air into the throat, with the help of the diaphragm, so that the stomach wall bounces outward and then
inward. Since such breaths may have a harmful effect on the
stability of the air supply, they should be taken only when
absolutely necessary.

When taking breath in the absence of a rest, one generally
shortens the note immediately preceding the breath by the
amount of time required for the breath itself, in order to avoid
interfering with the beat. Only in very quick passages is it
permissible to borrow time from the *following* notes. This
time must usually be paid back by playing these notes faster
than written, in order to catch up with the beat, which must
always be maintained, unless *musical*—not technical—considerations dictate otherwise. Needless to say, one usually
breathes between phrases, and seldom on the bar line or immediately before an accented note.[6]

It is useful to think of the air supply as a reservoir or as a
fuel supply, to be husbanded and used wisely, like any other
resource. The more depleted this reservoir becomes, the more
time and energy one must expend to refill it. Once the reservoir falls below a certain point, tone quality and steadiness of
tone deteriorate rapidly. Should one allow the reservoir to
drop still lower, it becomes impossible to refill to its proper
level without a lengthy pause, or an extended series of short
pauses. (Well-written woodwind music generally provides
such pauses at the ends of extremely long passages.) The
player who tries to do so by means of a string of quick, gasping breaths taken at inopportune moments only delays the
ultimate breakdown of his breath control, and makes his audience uncomfortable. Not only are such quick breaths generally insufficient for the replenishment of the air supply, but
they actually tend to make matters worse by disturbing the

---

[6] A full discussion of phrasing and other musical considerations governing the taking of breath lies beyond the scope of this book. Such discussions may be found
in Quantz, pp. 87-90, and Rockstro, pp. 501-507.

operation of the player's respiratory tract (as has already been noted above). The ability to play long uninterrupted passages all in one breath hinges as much on careful preparation and planning as on pure physical stamina. It is the player's responsibility to regulate the size and frequency of his breaths according to the music, so that his reservoir of air becomes neither too full nor too depleted. Obviously, long phrases demand deep breaths, while a succession of short phrases calls for a series of relatively shallow breaths. One must guard against expending one's air too freely, especially during the performance of the first half of a lengthy passage. Such passages need to be played relatively softly, in order to conserve breath. All this must, of course, be accomplished without compromising musical considerations of phrasing, articulation, and dynamic level. With regard to these last two, it will be obvious that the greater the degree of legato and volume, the more air will be required. Seldom, however, does physical exhaustion become the sole reason for taking a breath in recorder-playing, if the player manages his air supply properly.

To develop breath control, and tone in general, the practice of long tones is essential. One should sustain different notes without vibrato as long as possible, after taking a full breath, noting the point at which the tone becomes unsteady. It should be the concern of the player to try to avoid letting his reservoir of air drop below this point when executing a piece of music. With this in mind, the experienced player breathes wherever the opportunity presents itself, whether or not he needs the air (e.g., whenever a rest occurs, in most instances). By taking many breaths of moderate length where the music permits, he creates the illusion of long phrases and excites admiration for the power of his lungs, which less experienced players attempt in vain to gain through sheer physical stamina.

SOME PRECAUTIONS FOR PUBLIC PERFORMANCE

Observance of the principles of good breath control outlined above becomes all the more essential in public performance, when nervousness causes the pulse to quicken, the
blood pressure to rise, and the lungs to quake. These and
other physiological changes increase the metabolism, and
hence the amount of air needed to satisfy the basic vital (non-
musical) functions, while at the same time they decrease the
capacity of the lungs. The rate of respiration increases as the
lungs rid themselves of excess carbon dioxide. The air within
them becomes more rapidly vitiated at the very time when
they are called upon to exercise the most delicate control of
the airstream. At the same time, the amount of air needed by
the instrument remains unchanged, and thus actually decreases in proportion to the air needed for maintenance of
the player's vital functions. The air in the lungs tends to grow
stale *before* the time comes for the next breath. This induces
feelings of panic which, combined with other nervous mani-
festations, may threaten to disrupt the performance. These
symptoms, frightening though they are to inexperienced
players, can be minimized and controlled in several ways. The
performer should sit quietly for at least thirty minutes before
a concert to lower his metabolism as much as possible. He
should refrain from eating heavily before a performance,
since a full stomach makes proper breath control more difficult. The necessity for a long moment of preparation before
beginning to play has already been mentioned. The taking of
a sufficient number of breaths of the proper size assumes great
importance, along with the observance of the correct sequence
of steps in inhaling and exhaling. Should the player nevertheless feel himself choking on his own vitiated air (as may
sometimes happen despite all precautions), he may resort to
the emergency expedient of releasing some of this excess air

through the nose while playing, in order to relieve the pressure and make room for a greater amount of fresh air when the next breath is taken. (On the piccolo recorder [sopranino], this technique may be considered standard operating procedure, particularly in Vivaldi's three well-known concertos for that instrument, along with the practice of ventilating the lungs by rapidly breathing in and out several times during long rests.) Other than this, there is no sure remedy but experience. The player should seize every opportunity to perform. The seasoned performer regards his body as a tool, like his instrument. He learns how to use it as best he can. He discovers how it responds to stress, and how he may employ some of its responses to good advantage. He maintains an almost religious sense of separation between his self (or his soul, perhaps) and his physical being. He refuses to be defeated by the latter's limitations, just as he refuses to accept the supposed limitations of his instrument. He cares enough about his art to prepare rigorously for every concert; yet he maintains sufficient sense of proportion and confidence to take mistakes—and even disasters—in his stride. It may be helpful for the inexperienced performer to pretend to be playing at a rehearsal, rather than at a concert. Indeed the truly dedicated musician may well come to believe that the distinction between rehearsal and performance is largely an artificial one. He will begin to regard his concerts as rehearsals in preparation for still higher levels of achievements, while at the same time taking his rehearsals more seriously. If he is inspired more by a love of music than by a desire for applause, he will recognize that a musician's real triumphs may occur in private practice as well as in the concert hall. If he relies on himself and on those whose honesty and judgment he respects for criticism, rather than on the public, he will become neither unduly elated nor inordinately depressed by the outcome of a performance. Such a combination of confidence and equanimity constitutes what is perhaps the best defense against nervousness. Even the best performers have their failures as well as their successes. Even if they fail, they will gain the respect and admiration of intelligent listeners, who are wise enough to appreciate the superiority of a brilliant failure over a mediocre success.

VIBRATO[7]

Vibrato consists of the production of regular, controlled, and more or less rapid oscillations in the pitch and intensity of the tone. On the recorder, as on the transverse flute, vibrato is normally produced by the action of the throat, *assisted* by, and *coupled* to, the pressure and muscular action of the diaphragm. The resulting oscillations in the strength of the airstream affect the pitch, volume, and intensity of the note. The preferred vibrato on recorder and flute involves both the diaphragm and the throat, rather than just the diaphragm alone, as is often asserted. The ancient finger vibrato or *flattement* has almost no practical value today, and need not concern us here.

In the generation of vibrato, the throat functions as a valve. The player causes the musculature of his throat to assume the proper degrees and attitudes of tension, relaxation, and constriction, so that the flow of diaphragm-impelled air causes the effective diameter of the trachea alternately to expand and contract many times in succession, thus causing the strength of the airstream to increase and diminish in quick, regularly-spaced cycles. This valvelike action of the throat apparently results not from any muscular contractions, but rather from the physical aerodynamic effects of the passage of air through a narrow tube with springy, flexible walls. The process bears a resemblance to the regular interruptions of the airstream that occur when one blows through the sev-

[7] The present discussion of vibrato owes much to Roger S. Stevens' brilliant analysis of the subject (Stevens, pp. 41-44), to which the reader is referred.

ered mouthpiece and neck of a toy balloon. (Only a pure diaphragm vibrato involves rhythmic muscular movements; but
this form of vibrato is useless, except as a pedagogical aid.
Failure to appreciate the passive role of the muscles of the
respiratory tract in vibrato generation causes students to
tense these muscles unecessarily and constitutes one of the
main obstacles in the development of a fine tone.) The diaphragm serves mainly to cushion and smooth out the oscillations produced in the throat. It also plays a role in their generation, in conjunction with the throat, not only by exerting
the proper amount of pressure, but also by being free to
move in phase or sympathy with the resultant oscillations (as
may sometimes happen in the most intensely-played high register tones). The vibrato-generating process appears to resemble the actions of the throat and diaphragm in coughing,
laughing, and grunting. Acting in conjunction with one another, the throat and the diaphragm control the frequency,
amplitude, regularity, and contour of the vibrato oscillations.
The techniques for this control are more easily learned than
analyzed.

If represented graphically, a correctly-produced vibrato
would appear as a sine wave, with the abscissa signifying the
passage of time and the ordinate changes in pitch and intensity. The oscillations would probably extend a greater distance above than below the perceived pitch of the note.

The necessity for the coupling of the diaphragm to the
throat in the production of vibrato (in much the same way
as the air-reed is coupled to the air column in the production
of the tone) must be emphasized. A pure throat vibrato is almost always unacceptable on account of the extreme rapidity
and jagged profile of its oscillations, plus its inherently uncon-
trollable and mechanical nature. (I have only once heard a
recorder played with a beautiful throat vibrato.) It seems
more suited to the bleating of a goat than to the enhancement
of the tone of a recorder or transverse flute. On the other

hand, a pure diaphragmatic vibrato seems even more unsuited for use on the recorder by virtue of its extreme slowness.

The mastery of vibrato poses many difficulties. There are, however, several exercises to facilitate the process. The student should first learn to produce a pure diaphragm vibrato *away* from the recorder by saying "uh-uh-uh-uh" or "ah-ah-ah-ah" (as when laughing, groaning, coughing, or grunting), in a deep, resonant voice, from the bottom of the chest. It should be possible to see and feel the slow pulsations at the stomach wall. After accomplishing this, one may proceed to whisper the above-mentioned syllables while playing long tones in the second octave. (c''' is a good note on which to begin.) The resultant vibrato should have the profile of a slow sine wave, free from any unevenness or any abrupt changes in pitch and intensity. Once this has been accomplished, an attempt should be made to increase the oscillation frequency little by little, so that the throat begins to oscillate in place of the diaphragm, while the latter muscle provides the requisite support. The student should practice increasing the vibrato frequency while sustaining a single tone, in imitation of a steam locomotive pulling out of a station. One should strive to attain a speed of four evenly-spaced oscillations per beat, at a metronome setting of 76-80. Having achieved this in the middle register, one may then work one's way up and down the scale, always using the metronome, falling back on the above-mentioned exercises when necessary. Careful practice of this routine, together with attention to the maintenance of proper diaphragmatic support of the tone, as described earlier in this chapter, will do much to facilitate the development of a good vibrato. Above all, the player must avoid tensing the diaphragm or tightening the throat. He should cultivate the ability to perceive improvement or deterioration in his tone, and to relate such changes to an awareness and memory of his precise physical and mental attitudes at every moment of his practice. In addition to a good ear, a powerful imagination, an analytical self-awareness, and an enormous reserve of patience and perseverance, the assistance of a good teacher can be of enormous help in the development of a good vibrato.

Vibrato should be used to enhance a beautiful tone, rather than to mask a poor one. The attitude of determined support which characterizes the respiratory tract of a good recorderist during performance should always be present whether or not one plays with vibrato. It is difficult, if not impossible, to lay down rules for the employment of vibrato. In general, all tones occupying a space of two or more of the fastest oscillations which the player can produce should be played with vibrato, unless musical considerations make it inadvisable to do so. Notes shorter than this, and all double-tongued notes, are usually best played without vibrato, lest the oscillations be perceived as errors in intonation, rather than as expressive inflections in timbre and intensity. Short detached notes usually demand a faster vibrato frequency and greater amplitude than longer tones and slurred passages of several notes. Very short tones may be played with a pure throat vibrato, with a frequency too fast to be sustained for more than a fraction of a second. Very long tones may generally be played with vibrato of low amplitude, vibrato of gradually increasing amplitude, or even no vibrato at all, as musical considerations and taste dictate. The amplitude and frequency of vibrato usually, but not always, vary directly with the dynamic level and degree of intensity, except as noted above. Indeed, vibrato may be used to create the illusion of dynamic inflection. Appoggiaturas and other notes which receive a stress are often played with more vibrato than notes on weak beats. Sometimes, however, appoggiaturas may be executed loudly and without any vibrato (which must then be introduced on their resolution) to accentuate their harsh dissonant quality. Slow movements generally call for more vibrato than fast ones. One usually employs a faster vibrato for fast movements than for slow ones. Other and more subtle uses of vibrato may be gleaned from the performances of good singers and instrumentalists, particularly transverse flutists, and from experimentation and the creative use of one's own imagination.

Vibrato frequency may be either measured or unmeasured, depending on the circumstances, the main consideration being that it sound as a natural part of the tone, rather than as something superimposed on it. A measured vibrato (that is, one with a consciously fixed number of oscillations per beat) is often employed when playing with another recorder or with a transverse flute. It is also used frequently in dance-like pieces with a lively rhythm.

The higher registers (above g''') are usually played with very little vibrato. It is in this range that the relationship of the recorder to its offspring, the clarinet, becomes especially explicit.

SOME REMARKS ON INTONATION

Vibrato causes the apparent pitch of a note to rise. It thus constitutes a means of pitch control. A note played without vibrato should be blown harder, or otherwise rendered sharper in pitch, than the same note played with vibrato. Double-tongued passages, being played always without vibrato, tend to sound flatter than passages of slower notes. For this reason, it may occasionally be advisable to push in the tuning joint slightly for fast movements and to pull it out for slow ones, particularly when playing pieces that have long passages of double-tongued notes in the low and lower-middle registers.

When tuning the recorder to other instruments, it is best to use two notes as references, rather than just the a'', which is by no means the recorder's most stable note. (The most reliable note for tuning is usually c'''.) I make use of c''' and a'', tuning the recorder so that the former sounds slightly flat and the latter slightly sharp. The recorder's inherent intonational flexibility, the greater ease with which most of its notes can be raised rather than lowered in pitch, the tendency of its pitch to rise during performance, the desirability of producing a full, strong tone, the player's relative insensitivity to sharpness rather than flatness,[8] and the listener's greater sensitivity to sharpness rather than flatness—all these factors make it desirable to tune the recorder slightly flat, adjusting the pitch upward as one plays, rather than to make a futile attempt to match the pitch of the other instruments exactly. In tuning, one must take care to blow as hard as one does in actual performance. Failure to observe this precaution renders the instrument sharp.

For public performance, one should take care to tune the harpsichord slightly flatter than the recorder's highest attainable pitch, since under certain conditions, the pitch of the harpsichord may tend to rise during a concert.

It should be emphasized that the recorder is naturally out of tune. This is particularly true of the bell-keyed recorder, which is as hard to play in tune as the baroque one-keyed transverse flute. The recorderist must take pains to minimize the intonational defects of his instrument, through the employment of the proper techniques of pitch adjustment. At the very least, harmonic tones, tones of structural importance, sustained notes, accented notes, and other prominent tones ought to be in tune as much as possible. The same goes for all notes in unison passages. Other notes (such as unaccented passing tones) permit greater leeway in intonation.

---

[8] For a discussion of this problem as it applies to the transverse piccolo, see Stevens, p. 108.

CHAPTER V

The Operation of the Speaker-Vents and the Control of Intonation

PRELIMINARY REMARKS

On the transverse flute, the embouchure plays a major role in register selection (or "octaving"), and intonation control. By varying the size, shape, and angle of the airstream, the transverse flutist determines which of several possible registers will sound with a given fingering. By means of these same techniques, and also by covering more or less of the embouchure hole with the lips, he also controls intonation, and hence, dynamic inflection, since all flutes rise in pitch when blown loudly and drop in pitch when blown softly, unless this effect is compensated for. The flutist also controls timbre by adjusting the embouchure. The recorderist, by virtue of the recorder's fixed flue, is denied the use of the embouchure for these purposes, except to a very limited degree. He must therefore resort to other means of exercising this control, without which the recorder's powers of expression would be greatly curtailed. The partial opening of the upper-most tone-holes through pinching and half-holing, and the judicious use of alternate fingerings constitute these other means of control. The left thumb and fingers of the recorder-ist take over most of the duties performed by the flutist's lips.

PINCHING AND HALF-HOLING

On the recorder, register-selection and the adjustment of intonation and timbre fall largely under the control of the speaker-vents.[1] The speaker-vents are defined as openings whose size may be varied at will to facilitate the formation of antinodes (for register selection), and/or to vary the imped-ance for intonation control.[2] For purposes of the present dis-cussion, only those openings made by uncovering all or part of holes 1, 2, and 3 will be considered as speaker-vents. However, it should be borne in mind that other holes may occasionally perform this function. For example, since the uncovering of hole 4 as part of both the standard keyless fingering for e''' and the fingering for b''' causes the formation of an antinode, the opening thus formed constitutes a speaker-vent.

The most important speaker-vents are those formed by the partial opening of hole 1 with the left thumb. The tech-niques for forming and controlling these openings are collect-ively known as "pinching." The partial opening of holes 2 and 3 to cause the formation of additional speaker-vents is

[1] I resort to the term "speaker-vents" as the nearest analogy to "speaker-keys," to which the speaker-vents are identical in principle and function. The term "speaker-hole" would be misleading, since it implies a fixed opening, which is, by its very nature, contrary to the underlying principles of recorder technique.

[2] For a discussion of the terms "antinode" and "impedance," see Philip Bate, *The Oboe*, pp. 119-127.

called "half-holing." There are three types of pinching: first-position, second-position, and half-position.

First-position Pinching

This is the oldest and most basic of the three types of pinching. It consists of the insertion of the thumbnail into the upper edge of the thumbhole in order to form a crescent-shaped opening, which will be referred to as the first-position crescent or upper crescent. This is accomplished by bending the thumb inward at the lowest knuckle (which forms the principle pivot for this movement) so that the lower phalanx of the thumb points away from, and in front of, the player. The upper phalanx and metacarpal bone of the thumb necessarily move upward during this motion, pivoting on their joints, so that the position of the left hand is not displaced or disturbed during pinching. When shifting from a closed thumbhole to a pinched thumbhole fingering, the thumb must always remain in contact with the recorder. The necessity for adhering to the left-hand position described in Chapter II must be emphasized. Only this position allows the borders of the upper crescent to be defined and controlled exclusively by the stronger, more central portion of the thumbnail, rather than by the cuticle and the weakest part of the thumbnail. (See p. 23)

Variation in the size of the first-position crescent constitutes one of the principal means of controlling register selection. First-position pinching may be compared to the principal speaker-key of the clarinet. It is usually not necessary to press the thumbnail against the inner edge of the thumbhole with any force; nevertheless the constant friction of the thumbnail against the thumbhole necessitates repeated re-bushing of the thumbhole with ivory. An ivory thumb-bushing may last anywhere from one to two years. Needless to say, the size and shape of the thumbnail must be carefully regulated by means of a nail file. In general, the optimum length of the thumbnail increases slightly as the thumb-bushing wears down.

First-position pinching finds its most useful employment in the middle range of the recorder. Each note has its own optimum first-position crescent size for a given dynamic level, at least in theory—although first-position pinching plays only a secondary role in pitch adjustment in most registers, and hence in dynamic variation. However, the pitch (and therefore the dynamic level) of conventionally-fingered e‴ may be controlled by diminishing the size of the first-position crescent in the forte (thus flattening the pitch), and increasing its size in the piano (thus sharpening the pitch). Certain other notes are susceptible to such control to varying degrees. Notes of the lower-middle register (i.e., below c♯‴) are affected very little by it.

When slurring upwards from conventionally-fingered d‴ to conventionally-fingered e‴, the first-position crescent should be kept small, lest the e‴ refuse to sound.

In the first or low register, first-position pinching constitutes the most important technique for achieving a pianissimo. The opening of a small first-position crescent not only causes the pitch to rise (thus allowing the note to be played much softer); it also weakens the intensity of the tone. With the aid of first-position pinching, the recorderist can achieve crescendos and diminuendos of the kind so admired on the transverse flute and other instruments. It is particularly effective to employ this technique on the final note of a piece, to make the note "die away."

Despite its importance, first-position pinching does not give sufficient control over register selection as one ascends into the higher registers. To achieve such control, it becomes necessary to resort to other techniques.

Second-position Pinching[3]

To execute second-position pinching, one continues the bending of the thumb (as described above), while at the same time pushing upward with the thumbnail so that the fleshy ball of the thumb rolls away from the bottom of the thumb-hole, thus opening a second crescent-shaped aperture. This constitutes the second-position crescent or lower crescent. It exercises supplementary control over register selection in the recorder's upper range. It helps control pitch and timbre in the middle and upper registers. Without second-position pinching, it is virtually impossible to play softly in the third octave. In second-position pinching, the upper surface of the thumbnail constitutes the principal—and often the sole—point of contact between the left thumb and the recorder. In the fifth register, the player must often press the thumbnail's upper surface against the edge of the hole with considerable force, in order to bend it and thus achieve the correct adjustment in the size of the two pinching crescents. Some physical discomfort may be experienced, especially if the thumbhole is rather small.

The first position crescent's main function is the control of register selection. It acts as an octaving device. The second-position crescent also controls register selection, particularly in the upper registers, where the formation of two speaker-vents with the left thumb greatly facilitates the production of most of the notes between $c\sharp'''$ and c'''', inclusive.[4] But it also serves to control intonation and timbre, in conjunction

---

[3] The earliest reference to this technique of which I am aware is contained in A. Rowland-Jones, *Recorder Technique*, p. 95.

[4] It is interesting to note that similar speaker-vents have been introduced at various times on the transverse flute, and are still in use on the transverse piccolo and the newly-revived conical Boehm flute. See Rockstro, pp. 182-183, 315.

with half-holing. Enlargement of this crescent causes the pitch of many notes above c''' to rise, and enables them to be blown more gently, and hence more softly. At the same time, it lends them an ethereal quality, especially when used simultaneously with half-holing.

Needless to say, the possible variations in the actual and relative size of the two crescents are infinite. Each note requires a particular pinching configuration at any given dynamic level. The player must discover for himself what works best for each note on his particular instrument.

In general, precision in pinching tends to become more critical as one ascends. It should be noted that d'''' and certain other very high notes respond best to first-position, rather than second-position pinching.

Half-position Pinching

If the player bends his thumb as if executing first-position pinching, while at the same time shifting it slightly downward so that a crescent-shaped opening appears at the upper edge of the thumbhole *without* the thumbnail touching the recorder, he will have executed half-position pinching. Half-position pinching may be considered an abbreviated form of first-position pinching, in which the crescent is defined by the fleshy part of the thumb, rather than by the thumbnail. Its use is very restricted. It may be used in moderately fast passages involving leaps between a low register note and a middle register note below c#''', in which circumstances permit wide latitude in the size of the crescent, and nothing is to be gained from the extra effort required for true first-position pinching.

It should be emphasized that the experienced player is seldom conscious of the distinctions between the three pinching positions described above. He tends to view them as points along a gradient or continuum, as is also the case with the embouchure and the tongue-stroke. Thus, it will seldom be necessary to notate these positions specifically in the table of fingerings. Should the occasion arise, the following symbols may be employed:

For pinching, the specific position not specified: $\underline{1}$.
For first-position pinching: $1'$ (or 1^1).
For second-position pinching: $1''$ (or 1^2).
For half-position pinching: $\boldsymbol{\underline{1}}$.

In theory, two other pinching positions are possible. The first of these would involve the formation of the second-position lower crescent without the uncovering of the first-position crescent. This must be rejected, since it denies the player positive control over register-selection without offering any advantage. The second would consist of the formation of the half-position upper crescent by bending the thumb *outward*, in the direction opposite that recommended above. This must also be rejected, since it requires more effort than half-position pinching, offers no particular advantage, and places the thumb in an attitude from which the three recommended pinching positions become more difficult to assume.

Half-holing

Half-holing consists of the partial uncovering of a hole other than the thumbhole, in order to form a speaker-vent for control of intonation, dynamic level, and/or timbre. Half-holing also plays a secondary role in register selection, in conjunction with pinching. The partial uncovering of a hole as part of a regular fingering (e.g., hole 7 when fingering $c\sharp''$) will be called half-stopping, rather than half-holing, to avoid confusion. Half-holing is notated by the underlining of the numeral of the hole in question. Thus, its notation is identical to that of pinching, to which it is closely related.

To half-hole, one moves the finger *downward* from the knuckle (towards the foot of the instrument) while keeping the soft fleshy pad in contact with the wood. The finger will roll away from the hole, exposing a crescent-shaped opening that can be controlled with great precision. As in pinching, widening the opening formed by the partial uncovering of the hole raises the pitch of the note.

Hole 2 offers the most useful opportunities for half-holing. On the bell-keyed recorder, the conventional keyless fingerings for c#''', d''', f''', and certain other notes must be half-holed (and often played with second-position pinching as well) except in fast passages, if they are not to sound uncomfortably flat.[5] Below c''', the half-holing of 2 ceases to be effective in raising the pitch, and it becomes necessary to resort to half-holing of 3 (for keyless-fingered b'', b♭'', and a'') and even 4 (for a♭''). However, bell-keyed b'' responds somewhat to 2, while second-register g'' responds to 2 and 3. f'' may be sharpened with 2, and first-register g'' by means of 3. When using 3 and 4 to sharpen a''' (1 3 4 6 ½7 X), and indeed whenever half-holing on 4, it is necessary to roll the finger sideways (rather than up and down in the usual manner) towards the player's left, thus reducing the degree of its positive curvature.

Half-holing offers the player control over timbre as well as intonation. The ethereal quality of many half-holed notes has already been noted. A properly constructed bell-keyed recorder will require almost constant half-holing in the second octave, except when it is played loudly. This peculiarity of construction serves to maximize the dynamic range, by making possible a louder fortissimo. It is one of the chief advantages of the bell-keyed recorder over the conventional recorder.

Half-holing is indispensible for proper control of the middle and upper registers. Its specific applications, in con-

---

[5] It should be noted, in passing, that this technique of half-holing with the left index-finger, though used on the oboe and even the recorder in the eighteenth-century (see Dale S. Higbee, "Third-Octave Fingerings in Eighteenth-Century Recorder Charts," *The Galpin Society Journal*, Vol. XV [March 1962], pp. 98-99), was apparently unknown on the one-keyed flute, on which it offers a useful method of sharpening the normally flat f#'' and improving the speech of d#'' and e''.

junction with pinching, for the control of register selection, are so varied that no attempt can be made to codify them. As with pinching, the more sophisticated applications of half-holing must be discovered by the individual player through experience with his individual instrument. However, some of the specific uses of this technique have been indicated in the table of fingering in Chapter VII.

Mastery of half-holing may be facilitated by the practice of "warble tones," in which one produces a regular oscillation in pitch through variation of the size of the appropriate half-hole speaker-vent while sustaining a tone with absolutely no breath vibrato. A frequency of one oscillation per count at a metronome setting of 116 is recommended.

The "echo key" or "piano key," invented by Dr. Carl Dolmetsch, constitutes an additional speaker-vent comparable to those speaker-vents formed by half-holing. I have not used this device, which would seem to have great potential despite its "either-or" nature, as a means of obtaining dynamic variation, particularly in the low register, where half-holing is impossible on most notes. However, it seems undesirable to have such a key under the control of the chin, rather than the left hand.

THE USE OF ADDITIONAL HOLES, AND OF DUPLICATE FINGERINGS, FOR INTONATIONAL CONTROL

Each fingering has its own potential dynamic range and timbre. The recorderist is fortunate in that his instrument has a large number of duplicate fingerings, some of which are of great practical importance. A number of these are simply derivatives or variations of basic fingerings. Others are quite different. The discovery and use of these fingerings constitutes one of the means of controlling intonation, dynamic nuance, and timbre on the recorder. It is important to understand the principles behind such fingerings.

Most notes in the first or low register can be flattened
and rendered more reedy in timbre through the closure of
additional holes below the lowest closed hole of the regular
fingering. For example, c″ may be strengthened in this manner by closing hole 8 or the key, d″ by closing holes 6, ½7,
and the key, and e″ by closing hole 6. (These and other examples may be found in the table of fingerings.) This technique of closing additional holes finds a more limited application in the middle and higher registers. One may also half-
stop holes that are normally open. b♭′ may be reinforced by
half-stopping hole 6. Some players have suggested the use of
"shading" for reinforcement and flattening;[6] but this technique (in which the player holds a finger directly over, but
not on, its hole) lacks the virtue of positive control.

Most cross-fingered notes in the low register can be sharpened by uncovering all or part of the lowest closed hole.[7] This
technique has no practical value with plain-fingered notes.

Most plain-fingered notes in the lower register can be re-
placed by cross-fingerings, in order to produce a softer, more
veiled tone. The most useful of these have been listed in the
table of fingerings at the end of Chapter VII (pp. 81 ff.).

The selection of the proper fingering for a given situation
constitutes a musical problem as much as a purely technical
one. In a sense, there are no "alternate" fingerings on the recorder. There are, rather, numerous *duplicate* fingerings of
greater or lesser utility, which the player should have in his
fingering vocabulary, ready for use in conjunction with the
techniques discussed above.

[6] See Rowland-Jones, *Recorder Technique,* pp. 68-69.
[7] *Ibid.,* p. 69.

CHAPTER VI

Summary of Factors Governing Register Selection and Tone Quality. Some Additional Remarks on Tone

It would be well to summarize and elaborate upon some of the techniques discussed in the previous chapters, lest the reader perceive these techniques as a series of unrelated procedures, rather than as aspects of an integrated art.

As one ascends the scale, the strength of the tongue-stroke, the degree of constriction of the throat, and the height of the apparent point of origin of the tone in the respiratory tract increase. The absolute strength of the airstream probably increases somewhat, although its relative strength (in relation to the maximum amount of air the note will bear without cracking) decreases dramatically. As one ascends the scale, the vowel sound which one whispers while blowing changes gradually from "ah" in the low register to "ee" in the high registers. Meanwhile, pinching and embouchure become ever more critical, particularly at low dynamic levels. Second-position pinching and half-holing assume greater importance, not only for control of pitch, dynamic level, and timbre, but for register selection as well. The relative size of the second-position crescent decreases as one ascends from b♭''' to c♯''''.

The size of the oral cavity remains unchanged, except at low dynamic levels, and when one wishes to muffle the tone —and also, on some recorders, for extremely high notes such as d''''. At such times, one may close the jaw almost completely.

The tone of a properly played recorder lies midway between that of the transverse flute and that of the clarinet. It has more of an edge than the former, but more of a fluty quality than the latter. It should also have some of the aristocratic nasality of the clarinet's upper registers, as well as an undertone of tension and restlessness that is all its own. It is normally played with the same type of vibrato as the transverse flute. Needless to say, any of these qualities can, and should, be modified for musical purposes, as musical considerations dictate.

In order to realize these attributes, and to make his instrument heard in the concert hall, the recorderist should blow up, rather than down to, the note; i.e., instead of tuning sharp and blowing softly, he should tune flat and blow harder, correcting flatness of pitch by means of the speaker-vents, vibrato, harder blowing, and fingering, as required. The recorder is inherently a more brilliant, less pastoral instrument than the transverse flute (which deserves the appellation "flauto dolce" more than does the recorder); it will sound weak and colorless if treated in the same fashion as the flute.[1]

Good recorder-playing should represent the triumph of art over nature; for the recorder is an "artificial" instrument

---

[1] See Eric Halfpenny's review of *The Recorder and Its Music*, by Edgar Hunt, *Music and Letters*, Vol. LXIII, No. 3 (July 1962), p. 272. It must be noted that the flute, as remodeled by Boehm, is much less a pastoral instrument than the eighteenth-century one-keyed flute, which represents the technological counterpart of the bell-keyed recorder.

to a far greater degree than the flute.[2] It requires much effort from the player if it is to reveal its real possibilities. Its chief defects are its anti-vocal qualities. To overcome these defects, the player must strive to obtain the maximum possible dynamic and tonal nuances, as well as a pure vocal legato, when appropriate. These things are especially hard to realize on the recorder, with its cumbersome technique; hence the necessity of treating the instrument in an "artificial" fashion, in which one resorts to artifice in order to transcend its inherent limitations. Selection of suitable fingerings should be governed by the type of articulation required, as well as by other, more obvious factors; some slurs can only be executed with certain fingerings (as will be seen in the next chapter).

Above d''', the quality of the recorder's tone becomes more and more like that of the upper register of the clarinet. Consequently, the amplitude of the vibrato should often be decreased as one ascends into the third octave. Below d''', the recorder may be treated more like the transverse flute, as regards vibrato.

Relaxation of the cheek pockets makes the tone somewhat less intense.

Since most of the above-mentioned factors controlling register selection become increasingly critical as one ascends into the recorder's fifth register (the range between a''' and c''''), it therefore follows that mastery of this register will greatly facilitate the player's control over the instrument's entire range. The player should therefore devote a great amount of effort to the study of this register, even if he prefers to confine himself to the recorder's traditional eighteenth-century range for purposes of performance. The practice of long tones in this register is especially beneficial. An interesting exercise to promote the development of control in the higher registers (and a test of such control) is the playing

---

[2] I use the word "artificial" in its eighteenth-century sense, meaning "contrived with skill and art."

of the bugle-call "taps" in the key of E major, starting on the note b″. This may be done on bell-keyed and keyless recorders alike, since none of the notes involved requires the closing of the bell.

Finally, each note on the recorder should be regarded, from the technical point of view, not only as part of a larger whole, but as a world in itself. Just as the trombonist makes the necessary adjustments in the length of his slide in a deliberate, methodical manner, so must the recorderist adjust his embouchure, tongue-stroke, fingering, and other factors, to achieve the desired pitch and tonal effect. In this connection, the necessity for hearing each note and visualizing each fingering as one plays cannot be overemphasized.

CHAPTER VII

Fingering

THE ACTION OF THE FINGERS AND
THE DEVELOPMENT OF GOOD EXECUTION

In general, the fingers, like all other parts of the body, ought to be as relaxed as possible in recorder-playing. One should always employ the minimum amount of tension and effort, both mental and physical, necessary to do the job.

In order to minimize the strain on the muscles, nerves, and tendons associated with the movement of the fingers, it is advantageous to move them as slowly and as loosely as possible, especially in fast passages. The logic behind this apparent contradiction becomes clear when one analyzes the movement of the fingers in relation to the passage of time. For this purpose, one may make use of the following diagram:

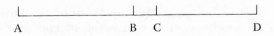

Line AD represents the passage of an interval in time. AB and CD constitute the amount of time necessary for two consecutive notes of the fastest possible Allegro, and BC represents the minute fraction of a second separating the two notes. All finger movements take place in the interval represented by line BC. It is with this period of time that we are chiefly concerned. It is assumed that the amount of time represented by BC is already so small that it is perceived by the listener as being instantaneous. Let it be understood that the ear is incapable of appreciating any differences in the rate of change of pitch that may occur within this space of time. The ear, in short, perceives BC as a point, rather than a line.

This being the case, it is self-evident that whether the finger movements occupy two-thirds or one-third of BC will have absolutely no effect upon the "neatness of execution," as perceived by the listener. However, since sudden, rapid movements place a greater strain upon the player's muscles, tendons, and nerves than slower movements (due to the effects of inertia and other physicochemical factors), it becomes clear that any decrease in the length of time within the space of BC devoted to finger movements will result in greater strain upon the player, and will thus interfere with the attitude of relaxed alertness that is so vital to good execution. These effects will be compounded in lengthy passages of rapid sixteenth-notes, in which the fatigue-inducing waste products of muscle movements and nerve impulses, which are produced in greater amounts by sudden rapid motions than by slower ones, have ample time to accumulate, in the course of the passage. (It is the cumulative effect of these fatigue-inducing byproducts of finger movements which causes the inexperienced player to collapse in the middle of a fast movement, by necessitating an ever-increasing amount of effort, until the breaking point is reached.) Conversely, any increase in the length of time devoted to finger movements must promote the attainment of good execution—provided, of course, that it remains within the time span represented by BC. The object of the player, then, must be to *maximize* the time span devoted to finger movements within these limits, so that the fingers move as slowly as possible, in order to expend the least possible energy, and thereby to decrease the production of fatigue-inducing waste products to a level at which they may be completely dissipated before the start of the next finger movement. In doing so, one must allow ample margin for the increased stress on the system that occurs during performance, and when the player is not feeling at his best.

There are several ways in which this may be accomplished. Firstly, one should keep the fingers rather close to the holes—about one half-inch away—particularly when performing stepwise passages. This will enable the fingers to move more slowly, since they will have less distance to travel. Secondly, one should exert little or no pressure on the holes, in order to promote relaxation and to minimize the work that must be performed by the muscles of the fingers. There should be little or no imprint of the holes upon the fleshy part of the fingers; a strong imprint indicates too much pressure. (See Chapter II, p. 21.) A minimum amount of pressure, coupled with a maximum amount of relaxation, promotes proper closure of the holes, by allowing the soft fleshy finger-pads to conform to the curved, rigid surface of the recorder. The fingers should be regarded not as little hammers, but as delicate electrical switches, which must merely make contact with their holes in order to produce the desired note. (These remarks do not apply to the left thumb during pinching: see the remarks on second-position pinching in Chapter V.) They should rise and fall with a minimum amount of weight or force. In order to relax the fingers and prepare them for their movements, it may be helpful for the student to crumple a sheet of newspaper in either hand.

The cultivation of good practice habits over a sustained period of time constitutes the third way of minimizing finger velocity and developing good execution. A practice session should never be continued beyond the point at which fatigue begins to manifest itself. One should avoid playing with aching fingers. A series of half-hour practice periods spread over the course of a day or separated by rest periods is usually more beneficial than a single long uninterrupted practice session. During the intervals between practice sessions, a kind of "silent learning" seems to take place, in which the advances made during practice consolidate themselves, so that the following practice period often witnesses seemingly miraculous achievements of new levels of proficiency. Rest periods have a positive value in the development of technique and in the mastery of new pieces. Excessive practice is counterproductive.[1] When not playing the recorder (i.e., during most of one's waking hours), one may, however, benefit from the silent practice of scales, arpeggios, and the like. This involves the actual movement of the fingers and the imagining of the resultant pitches—all this *away* from the instrument. Such silent practice should be regarded as a game. Most of one's actual practice on the instrument should be intensive, concentrated, and unrelenting. A half-hour of such study has far more value than five hours of desultory "practice." Nevertheless, some time for "fooling around" should be set aside, not only to provide opportunities for discovery of new procedures and facts, but to stimulate the imagination and to keep alive the joyous, playful aspects of *playing* a musical instrument.[2]

Difficult passages—and all passages in the beginning—should be isolated (it is helpful to circle them in pencil) and practiced at slow speed. All difficult passages should be analyzed into a series of individual finger movements and studied, one pair of notes at a time. In doing so, one should first practice each finger motion at an artificially slow rate of speed, so that the transition from one note to the next becomes audible as a glissando. This develops a sense of the position of the holes in relation to the fingers. It promotes relaxation and instills a sense of the fluidity of finger movement so essential to good execution. It also fixes the finger movements in the

---

[1] *Cf.* Quantz's warning against excessive practice (Quantz, p. 118).

[2] *Cf.* Michael Vetter, p. 8.

player's memory, and provides opportunities for achieving perfect synchronization in multiple finger movements. After several minutes of such slow-motion practice, one may then attempt the finger change at a normally slow tempo. The next step is to increase the tempo, taking care never to force the fingers, until the desired rate of speed has been attained. Frequent returns to slower tempi, including the ultra-slow glissando tempo, are recommended, particularly at the start of each practice session. When each pair of notes has been mastered, one may then repeat the whole procedure with four-note groups, eight-note groups, and finally, with entire passages. A mirror and a metronome constitute invaluable aids in following this routine. One should regard each note as a separate entity (see Chapter VI), and each passage as a series of distinct finger-changes, alternating with periods of rest (represented by the notes themselves), during which the fingers should be *completely relaxed.* Under no circumstances should the player regard a passage as an uninterrupted, amorphous entity, as beginners often do.

Psychology constitutes an additional aid in the development of good execution. The player, through concentration, coupled with and assisted by the practice methods outlined above, lengthens his subjective sense of time, so that each note and finger-change, however rapid it may be, seems to occupy a much greater time span in his mind than it actually does to the listener. This increased subjective perception of the passage of time gives the player time to think of the technical problems ahead, to plan accordingly, to observe the precepts of good fingering, and, above all, to relax.

When correctly executed, rapid step-wise passages seem to play themselves. The player feels as if he were drawing energy from the notes, rather than forcing the notes out of the instrument. It is almost as if one were bouncing a basketball. Just as the ball rebounds with a certain amount of energy which carries over to the next bounce, so that the basketball player need merely assist it with a slight tap, so does each finger movement of a properly executed rapid passage provide the impetus for the next. In both cases, one senses a certain rhythm, without which successful performance is impossible.

The execution of rapid arpeggiated passages involving many contrary finger movements, as well as some trills, demands certain departures from the principles outlined above. It often becomes necessary, in the case of the former, to lift the fingers rather high above their holes.[3] In extreme cases, if all else fails, the employment of tension may be necessary. However, such instances should be kept to a minimum, and the hand should be consciously relaxed afterwards. Similarly, some trills may require the tensing of the fingers.[4] Most players trill better with the fingers of one hand than the other. One should avoid forcing the speed of the trill, particularly when trilling with the weaker hand.

The half-stopping of the two double holes (holes 7 and 8) requires that the right wrist be rotated slightly counter-clockwise. To re-cover one or both holes entirely, one rotates the right wrist clockwise. In both cases, the pad of the finger involved may be allowed to slide over its double hole, though this is frequently unnecessary in the case of the smaller recorders. The semitone trills on f′ and g′ and the whole-tone trill on f♯′ are executed by rocking the lowest joint of the proper right-hand finger back and forth, so that the fleshy pad rolls on and off the more distant of the double-holes. Certain other otherwise impossible trills may also be performed in this manner. Except for these, and for the motions involved in pinching,[5] all finger movements should occur at the knuckles (as has already been noted in Chapter II).

When slurring across a register break, the fingers should move more slowly than usual, in order to match the relatively slow response of the air column to shifts in register. This applies equally to the pinching movements of the thumb.

---

[3] I am grateful to Samuel Baron for this suggestion.

[4] See Quantz, p. 37.

[5] See Chapter V, pp. 61 ff.

THE FINGERINGS OF THE BELL-KEYED,
COMPROMISE, AND KEYLESS RECORDERS

Except as indicated, the fingerings listed below apply equally to the bell-keyed, compromise, and keyless recorders. This list consists almost exclusively of fingerings that are of practical value; however, in a few cases, fingerings of great theoretical interest have been included as well. Duplicate fingerings exist for almost all notes of the recorder. An attempt has been made to indicate the relative importance of such fingerings by the use of Roman numerals; however, it should be understood that the nature of the recorder's fingering system makes such a classification only an approximation at best and an outright distortion at worst. The concept of "standard" fingerings is of doubtful value for all woodwinds; it is of virtually no value on the recorder, an instrument with a very rich vocabulary of fingerings. On the recorder more than any other woodwind, selection of fingerings influences volume, timbre, and other qualities generally subsumed under the heading of "expressivity." Although there are no "standard" fingerings in the broadest sense of the term, there do exist fingerings which are more or less standard for a given musical-technical situation. The selection of the proper combination of fingerings to achieve the desired result constitutes the grammar of recorder fingering; it is this, rather than the mere unorganized knowledge of scores of different fingerings, that represents a true understanding of fingering on the recorder.

The general principles governing fingering selection on the transverse flute have been brilliantly set forth by Rockstro in his *Treatise on the Flute*. They are equally valid for the recorder:

I. Never use different fingerings, which cause an alteration of pitch, for similar notes that are near each other [unless, as frequently is the case on the recorder, one wishes to make use of such pitch differences to achieve dynamic variation].

II. Do not select a sharp fingering for one note, and a flat fingering for another which is adjacent to it, but on the contrary, choose a set of sharp, or a set of flat notes, so that all may be corrected together by a slight change in the method of blowing.

IV [sic]. For slow music, select the fingerings which give the best notes, no matter how difficult they may be. Indifferent notes may occasionally be tolerated in very rapid passages, for the sake of smoothness and facility.

V. Avoid all unnecessary changes. The chief object of extra fingerings being the preservation of smoothness, they will be needed comparatively seldom in *staccato* passages, for which many of them would indeed be wholly unfitted.

VI. [This applies to the use of harmonic fingerings, which are practically nonexistent on the recorder.]

VII. Any finger-holes may be kept closed during the performance of rapid passages, provided no appreciable injury to intonation or tone be caused by such closing.[6]

One might add the rather obvious observation that fingerings should be selected which require the fewest finger movements, especially those in contrary motion, in going from one note to the next, particularly in fast passages.

In the table below, the numbers indicate those holes of the recorder to be closed for each fingering. The holes of the recorder are numbered 1 through 8, starting with the thumbhole. X indicates the closing of the bell by means of the bell key, or, in the case of the keyless recorder (and on the bell-keyed recorder when the right-hand little finger is otherwise occupied, unless the instrument is equipped with a long bell key for the little finger of the left hand), by pressing the bell against the knee. A line under a numeral or under X indicates partial covering of the hole in question. This is known as "pinching," in the case of 1, and "half-holing" in the case of the other holes; for example, "2" should be read as "two

---

[6] Rockstro, p. 457. Quoted by permission of the publisher, Musica Rara, London. Copyright © 1967 by Musica Rara.

half-holed." (Half-holing of the bell is accomplished by partial closure of the bell key.) 1 indicates pinching, the exact
pinching position unspecified. 1′, 1″, and *1* indicate first-
position, second-position, and half-position pinching, respectively. A fraction before a number indicates that the hole in
question is to be partially stopped. The enclosure of a symbol
in parentheses indicates an optional covering or uncovering
of the hole, or a choice of variants which have been deemed
too closely related to be classified as a separate fingering. In
all but a few special cases, sharps have been regarded as identical to flats, and equal temperament has been assumed throughout.

Some trills require special fingerings, as indicated below.
However, the appoggiatura of the trill must almost invariably
be sounded with the most resonant, in-tune fingering, however awkward this may be.

Table of Fingerings

 a♯-b♭

I. 1 2 3 4 5 6 7 8 X
Of theoretical significance
only, on account of its soft-
ness; on some pseudo-replicas
of Baroque recorders, this fingering yields a′.

f′

I. 1 2 3 4 5 6 7 8

$f^{\sharp}{}'\text{-}g^{\flat}{}'$

I. 1 2 3 4 5 6 7 ½8

II. 1 2 3 4 5 6 7 X

Of very little practical use. Reedier and softer than $f^{\sharp}{}'$I.

g'

I. 1 2 3 4 5 6 7

II. 1 2 3 4 5 6 ½7 X

A soft fingering. Of no practical significance.

$g^{\sharp}{}'\text{-}a^{\flat}{}'$

I. 1 2 3 4 5 6 ½7

II. 1 2 3 4 5 6 ½7 ½8

Useful for the $g^{\sharp}{}'\text{-}f^{\sharp}{}'$ trill, in conjunction with $f^{\sharp}$ I. See the remarks on this trill at the end of the opening section of this chapter (p. 78).

I. 1 2 3 4 5 6

$a^{\sharp}{}'\text{-}b^{\flat}{}'$

I. 1 2 3 4 5 7 8

The standard "English fingering," devised by Arnold Dolmetsch in the early twentieth century, and distinguished from the "Baroque fingering," 1 2 3 4 5 7.

II. 1 2 3 4 5 (½)7

A soft fingering on the modern recorder. 1 2 3 4 5 7 was the standard fingering on the Baroque recorder, and must be used on some present-day pseudo-replicas of eighteenth-century recorders.

III. 1 2 3 4 5 6 B♭ key

A few experimental recorders have such a key. Useful for the b♭$'$-a$'$ trill, and as a loud fingering.

IV. 1 2 3 4 5 ½6

Useful for the b♭$'$-a$'$ trill. See p. 78.

b$'$

I. 1 2 3 4 6 7

Sometimes too sharp.

II. 1 2 3 4 6 7 (½)8

A loud fingering. To be used also on those instruments on which b$'$ I is too sharp.

III. 1 2 3 4 6 ½7

A soft fingering.

IV. 1 2 3 4 5 (B♭ key)

A very loud fingering. Especially useful on the piccolo recorder (sopranino), when one wishes to play b$'$ as loudly as possible.

V. 1 2 3 4 ½5 6

Useful for the trill with a$'$. See p. 78.

VI. 1 2 3 4 ½5 7 8

For the trill with a♯$'$ I. See p. 78.

c″

I. 1 2 3 4

II. 1 2 3 4 8

III. 1 2 3 4 X

IV. 1 2 3 4 7 X

V. 1 2 3 5 6 7 8

II, III, and IV are increasingly louder and reedier on the bell-keyed recorder. III and IV usually do not work well on the compromise recorder.

For the trills with d♭″ I and V.

c♯″-d♭″

I. 1 2 3 5 6 (½)7

Too sharp on some instruments unless 7 is completely closed, as it must be for the trill with c″ V.

II. 1 2 3 5 6

For use in rapid alterations with a′. To be avoided otherwise, except as a soft fingering.

III. 1 2 3 4 C♯ key

On recorders equipped with a C♯ key, this fingering should be used whenever possible, except in soft passages.

IV. 1 2 4 5 6 7 ½8

For the trills with d♯″ II, V, or VI. By alternately taking d♯″ first with VI and then with II or V, and c♯″ with IV, a so-called double trill can be produced.[7]

V. 1 2 3 5 6 8

For a trill with c″ V.

[7] See Baines, p. 104.

d″

I. 1 2 3

The standard fingering, especially on the keyless and compromise recorders. Tends to be sharp on the bell-keyed recorder.

II. 1 2 3 7 X

III. 1 2 3 6 ½7 X

IV. 1 2 3 7 8

V. 1 2 3 6 (8)

II-V are louder and reedier than I. Their quality and utility vary greatly from one instrument to the next. They are usually preferable to I on the bell-keyed recorder.

VI. 1 2 4 5 6 ½7

Indispensable for the trill with e♭″ I.

VII. 1 3 4 5 6

Sometimes useful for the *Nachschlag* of the f″ I-e″ IV trill.[8]

d#″-e♭″

I. 1 2 4 5 ((½)7)

Often flat and harsh.

II. 1 2 4 6 7 ½8

Sometimes more refined in timbre and better in tune than I.

III. 1 3 4 5

A soft fingering. Useful in conjunction with f″ I and e″ IV.

---

[8] The *Nachschlag* of a trill (also known as the afterbeat, termination, or suffix) consists of two notes—the first a half-step or a whole-step below the principal note of the trill, the second identical with the principal note—which are appended to the trill. (The term *Nachschlag* also denotes a short appoggiatura occurring *before* the beat, which need not concern us here.) Most cadential trills end with either *Nachschlags* or anticipations.

IV. 1 2 3 E♭ key.

The E♭ key, operated by the right-hand index finger, constitutes a very desirable addition to the instrument. This fingering recommends itself especially as an upper neighbor and as a passing tone between d″ and f″.

V. 1 2 4 5 7 ½8

VI. 1 2 5 6 7 ½8

See c♯″ IV.

e″

I. 1 2

II. 1 2 5 (6) (7) (X)

Louder and reedier than I.

III. 2 3 4 5

Useful in conjunction with c″ II, and as a soft fingering.

IV. 1 3 4

To be avoided whenever possible, except for trills, as a lower neighbor to f″ in rapid slurred passages, and, on some instruments, as a soft fingering.

f″

I. 1 3

II. 2 3 4

For use in conjunction with f♯″ I, and as a soft fingering.

III. 1 4 5 (7)

For the trill with e♭″ I.

f#″-g♭″

I. 2 3 (X)

Usually more or less flat, and therefore to be avoided in soft passages. The addition of the key makes its tone slightly reedier.

II. 1 (8 or X)

For use in trills in conjunction with e″ I, and as a loud fingering. The addition of "8 or X" is for support only, and constitutes one of the very few acceptable instances of buttress fingering.

III. 2 4 5 (7)

For use as a leading tone, a soft fingering and in the trill with g#″ V.

IV. 1 or 1 2 3 (4 or 4) 5 6 7 8

V. 1 2 or 2 3 4 5 6 7 X

VI. 1 or 1 3 (4 or 4) 5 6 7 8

VII. 1 or 1 3 (4 or 4) 5 6 7 X

This and the following fingerings for second-register f#″ are occasionally useful for trills and slurs in conjunction with appropriate fingerings for g#″ in order to avoid the register break. They may also be used as soft fingerings and for a change in timbre. Their intonation and speech may vary widely from one recorder to another. IV and V are particularly useful for trills with g#″VI and VII. VII may be used to advantage for the trill with g#″VIII, and for a change in timbre. Other variants of these fingerings are possible.

g″

I. 3 (6) (7)

The standard first-register fingering. Often sharp. To be used in slurs with other first-register notes. It may be sharpened by 3 and flattened by 2, or by the addition of 6 and 7, when a reedier note is desired.

II. 2 3 4 5 6 7 8

The standard second-register fingering. To be used in slurs with other second-register notes to avoid the register break. It is fuller in tone than I. It may be sharpened by 2 or 3, or by lifting off 3 entirely. This fingering is usually slightly flat and recommends itself as a loud fingering. Useful for the trill with a″ III.

III. 4 (5) (7)

A soft fingering. Also useful in the trill with f♯″ III, and in conjunction with f″ III.

IV. 1 2 3 4 5 6 7 ¼8

Of very little importance, but of some use as a soft fingering and for slurs with g′.

g♯″-a♭″

I. (3)4 5 6 7

3 should be uncovered only for the trill with g″ III.

II. 2 3 4 5 6 7

A loud fingering. Occasionally useful for a trill with g″ II.

III. 0 (8 or X)

A loud fingering. Useful for the trill with f#″ I. The closure of 8 or of X serves only for support.

IV. 1̲ 2 3 4 5 6 ½7

Useful as a soft fingering, and for occasional passages involving other fingerings with 1̲.

V. 2 4 5 6 7

Useful for the trill with f#‴ III, despite the register break.

VI. 1̲ 2 3 (4) 6 7 8

Useful for the trill with f#″ IV.

VII. 1̲ 2 3 (4̲ or 4) 5 6 7

Useful for the trill with f#″ IV, and a change in timbre and loudness.

VIII. 1̲ or 1 3 (4̲ or 4) 5 6 7

Useful as a soft or loud fingering (depending upon the degree of pinching and half-holing), and for the trill with f#″ VII.

a″

I. 1̲ 2 3 4 5 6   ⎫
II. (2) 3 4 5 6   ⎬

I or II should be used whenever possible; as a rule, use I with a fingering involving 1 or 1̲, and II when coming from a fingering in which the thumbhole is open. I matches the quality of other pinched fingerings more closely than II, which tends to sound less veiled. On some recorders, II may be sharper and less pure than I. 2 should be uncovered *only* for the trill with g#″ I.

III. (1) 2 3 4 5 7 8

Cross-fingered a″. Useful for the trills with b♭″I and g″II, for rapid slurred passages involving these notes, and for the execution of the *Nachschlag* of the c″II-b♭″I trill. The same observations on the omission of 1 in a″I and II apply to this fingering as well. 1 must be left off for the trill with g″II.

IV. 1 2 3 4 5 6 ½8

A loud fingering.

a♯″-b♭″

I. 1 2 3 4 5 7

The usual fingering, also known as "English fingering." May be flattened by closing ¼6 or ¼8.

II. 2 3 4 5 7

Windier and fuller than I. Useful mainly for a change in timbre.

III. 3 4 5 7

For the trill with a♭″ I.

IV. 1 2 3 4 5 ½7 ⎫
                  ⎬
V. 1 2 3 4 5 8 ⎭

The standard eighteenth-century fingerings. Useful as soft fingerings, at least in theory.

VI. 1 2 3 4 6 8

Useful as a soft fingering and, on some keyless recorders, for a trill with b″ I.

VII. 1 2 3 4 5 6 B♭ key

See a♯′-b♭′ III.

b″

I. <u>1</u> 2 3 4 6

The standard fingering on the keyless and compromise recorders. Tends to be somewhat weaker and less dynamically flexible than II. To be avoided on the bell-keyed recorder (and II or III used instead), in those keys in which c#‴ occurs.

II. <u>1</u> 2 3 4 5 X

III. <u>1</u> 2 3 4 5 7 X

These are equal in importance to I on the bell-keyed recorder, and on some compromise recorders. (They tend to be out of tune on many compromise recorders.) The standard fingering for b″ in B major and related keys in which c#‴ occurs. III is slightly flatter, and therefore louder, than II. III is useful in conjunction with a#″ I (as in trills), for the trill with c#‴ II, and for slurs to and from c#‴ II, d#‴ I, e‴ I, and f‴ III, to avoid the usual register break. See also pp. 9-10. II is used next to c′″ I and in conjunction with g″ I and d‴ I.

IV. <u>1</u> 2 3 4 5 6 7 X

Useful for a change in timbre as well as in the trill with c‴ III.

V. 1″ 2 4 5 7

Useful for the trill with a#″ I, especially on the keyless recorder. (On the bell-keyed and compromise recorders, this trill is best made with b″ III-

a#″ I.) To be avoided otherwise, as it is flat and does not
speak readily.

VI. 1 2 3 5 6

By alternately taking b″ with
this fingering and with I in
the trill with a″ I, a double
trill can be produced.

c‴

I. 1 2 3 4

II. 1 2 3 5 7

For the trill with b♭″ I, and,
in alternation with c‴ I, for
the double trill with b♭″ I.
For the trill with d♭‴ III.
When performing this trill on
the bell-keyed recorder, 1″
should be used.

III. 1 2 3 5 6 X

Often preferable to II on the
bell-keyed recorder for the
trill with d♭‴, in conjunction
with d♭‴ I, particularly when
this trill resolves by anticipa-
tion to d♭‴, rather than b♭″.
Also useful as a soft fingering.

IV. 1 2 3 4 ½7

Theoretically useful as a loud
fingering.

V. 1 2 3 4 6 7 X

Theoretically useful for a
change in timbre. Fairly loud,
unless sharpened by 2 and 3.

VI. 1 2 4 5 7 X

Theoretically useful as a soft
fingering.

c#′′′-d♭′′′

I. <u>1</u> 2 3 5 X

The preferred fingering on the bell-keyed recorder, particularly in the key of D major. Useful as a soft fingering on the compromise recorder, on which it is sharp. Useful next to b″ II and d″ I. See also p. 9.

II. <u>1</u> 2 3 5 7 X

The addition of 7 makes this fingering slightly flatter than I. Useful for the trill with b′′′ III on the bell-keyed and compromise recorders. Useful in slurs to and from e♭′′′ I and e′′′ I, and in conjunction with d′′′ II. See p. 10. Both I and II may serve as soft fingerings on the compromise recorder (on which II is preferable to I), as well as for the avoidance of the usual break between the conventionally-fingered second and third registers in slurred passages; but these fingerings are difficult to play in tune on a compromise recorder.

III. <u>1</u> 2 3 5

The standard fingering on the keyless and compromise recorders. If flat, it should be sharpened by <u>2</u> and/or 1″. To be avoided whenever possible on the bell-keyed recorder (on which it is about an eighth of a tone flat unless sharpened by the player), except in rapid passages when other fingerings would be hopelessly awkward.

IV. $\underline{1}$ 2 3 6

For the trill with b″ on keyless and compromise recorders; also when slurring the passages b″ I-c#‴ IV-d‴ III. To be avoided otherwise, except possibly as a soft fingering. Superfluous on the bell-keyed recorder.

V. $\underline{1}$ 2 3 4 C# key

See c#″-d♭″ III.

d‴

I. $\underline{1}$ 2 3 X

The preferred fingering on the bell-keyed recorder. Dynamically very flexible, with the help of 1″ and $\underline{2}$. Sharp on the compromise recorder.

II. $\underline{1}$ 2 3 7 X

Useful mainly in slurs to e♭‴I, e‴I, and f‴III, and in the trill with e‴ IV. See p. 10. The addition of 7 serves to stabilize the third register, preventing it from breaking downward in slurred passages, and thus interfering with the smooth transition between the notes. Sharp on the compromise recorder, though less so than I.

III. $\underline{1}$ 2 3

The standard fingering on keyless and compromise recorders. Inferior in quality and intonation on the bell-keyed recorder, on which it should usually be avoided, except in fast passages. However, when sharpened by 1″ and $\underline{2}$, it

serves as a very useful soft
fingering on the bell-keyed recorder with a distinctively
veiled timbre.

IV. $\underline{1}$ 2 3 4 (5) 6 7 ½8

Useful mainly for the trills
with e$^{b\,\prime\prime\prime}$ III and e$^{\prime\prime\prime}$ III.

V. $\underline{1}$ 2 3 ¼4 5 6 7 8

Useful in the trills with e$^{b\,\prime\prime\prime}$ IV
and e$^{\prime\prime\prime}$ V. The trill with e$^{b\,\prime\prime\prime}$
is best made with this finger-
ing; but the trill with e$^{\prime\prime\prime}$ usually works best when taken
with IV.

VI. $\underline{1}$ 2 3 4 5 6 7 (¾)8

Useful for a double trill with
e$^{b\,\prime\prime\prime}$ V-VI.

d$\sharp$$^{\prime\prime\prime}$-e$^{b\,\prime\prime\prime}$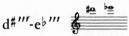

I. $\underline{1}$ 2 3 (5) 6 7

The principal fingering for this
note. Usually more or less
sharp, especially on the keyless and compromise recorders. The addition of 5 has very
little effect, other than chang-
ing the pitch of the "lower attendant sound";[9] it should
usually be left on, if only because it facilitates the change
to e$^{\prime\prime\prime}$ I. 5 should usually be
omitted in slurs from below,
and in pianissimo passages.

II. $\underline{1}$ 2 3 (5) 6 8

Very often the preferred fingering on the keyless recorder,
since it is flatter than I. Suit-

[9] See Rockstro, p. 74.

able as a loud fingering on the bell-keyed recorder. 5 is best left closed. Excellent for a trill with e''' I.

III. $\underline{1}$ 2 3 5·6 7 ½8

Flatter than II. The preferred fingering on some badly-constructed keyless recorders. Useful as a loud fingering, and in the trill with d''' IV.

IV. $\underline{1}$ 2 3 ¼4 5 6 7

Useful for the trill with d''' V.

V. $\underline{1}$ 2 3 5 6 7 (¾)8 ⎫
VI. $\underline{1}$ 2 3 4 5 6 7 ⎬   See d''' VI.
                          ⎭

VII. $\underline{1}$ 2 3 E♭ key.

Useful mainly for a trill with d''' III. Less useful than d#''- e♭ '' IV.

VIII. $\underline{1}$ 2 3 8

Very useful on some recorders, especially for a trill with d''' III, despite the register break. On many instruments, this fingering will not speak at all.

IX. $\underline{1}$ 2 4 5 6 7 ½8

Theoretically useful in conjunction with e''' III, as, for example, in trills. Also usable, though superfluous, as a soft fingering. Speaks with great difficulty.

e'''

I. $\underline{1}$ 2 3 5 6

The standard fingering. Its slight flatness on the bell-keyed recorder may be remedied by means of 2 and/or 1″. This fingering should usually be used in conjunction with f′′′ III. Avoid using it after f′′′ I. See also d′′′ II, and p. 10.

II. 1′ or 1, 2 3 (4) 5 6 7 X

Usually sharp, but clearer than I. 4 should generally be left open, except for a change in timbre. Useful in conjunction with f′′′ I, g′′′ I, and other fourth register notes, particularly in slurred passages, and for slurred leaps from below. It should never be used next to f′′′ III. Useful as a piano fingering. I is usually better in loud passages. This fingering possesses a very wide dynamic range and lends itself to a *messa di voce*. Complete closure of 1 makes it louder and better in tune, but also strengthens the lower attendant sound.

III. 1 or 1, 2 5 6 7 (½8)

Excellent for slurred leaps from below, and for a trill with d′′′ IV, provided that ½8 is left closed. This fingering has a wide dynamic range. Complete closure of 1, together with ½8, makes it a good loud fingering. Useful next to f′′′ I, provided that ½8 is left open.

IV. 1 2 3 7

See d′′′ II.

V. 1 2 3 ½4 5 6

See d′′′ V.

VI. 1″ 2 X

Useful on the bell-keyed and compromise recorders for a trill with d′″ I, although this trill is not very well in tune when made this way. Otherwise, speaks with some difficulty.

VII. 1″ 2

Useful for a trill with d′″ III on the keyless recorder only. Otherwise speaks with great difficulty. This trill is best made in one of the other ways given above.

f′″

I. 1 or 1, 2 (4) 5 6 7 X

The preferred fingering on bell-keyed and compromise recorders. Very wide dynamic range, controllable by pinching. Eminently suitable for a *messa di voce*. 4 should be left open, except for a trill with g♭′″ I, g′″ VII or VIII, or very loud passages.

II. 1 or 1, 2 4 6 7 X

Softer than I. For the softest possible pianissimo, by means of 1″ and 2. Can be used for a trill with g′″ IX, although the g′″ VIII-f′″ I trill is preferable.

III. 1 2 5 6

The standard fingering on the keyless recorder. Flat on the bell-keyed recorder and on some keyless and compromise recorders, unless sharpened by

1″ and/or <u>2</u>. A soft, sweet note. Useful even on the bell-keyed and compromise recorders for a change in timbre, and in conjunction with e‴ I and d‴ II.

f#‴-g♭‴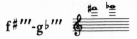

I. <u>1</u> <u>2</u> 4 5 7 X

The preferred fingering. It is ironic that this fingering, for which the bell key was originally invented, remains in need of the player's constant attention, lest it be flat. 4 may be left open for the trill with f‴ I. Very wide dynamic range. In the loudest passages 1 and 2 may be completely closed.

II. <u>1</u> 2 4 5 7 <u>X</u>

This is the fingering that usually results when one closes the bell of a keyless recorder on one's knee, since cloth, being porous, does not provide perfect closure of the bell hole. It is better in tune than I.

III. <u>1</u> 2 4 5 X

Sharp.

IV. 1″ <u>2</u> 4 6 X

Useful in conjunction with g‴ VII.

V. 1″ (4) 5 6 7 X

Of some use next to f‴ I, as in a trill.

VI. 1′ 2 (3) 4 5 6 8

The standard fingering on

the keyless recorder. To be avoided whenever possible, as it is always sharp. Useful next to g''' II.

VII. 1 2 3̲ 4 5 6 8

Preferable to VI, as it is better in tune, but awkward. Both this fingering and VI are obsolete on the bell-keyed and compromise recorders.

VIII. 1̲ 5 6

Useful for a trill with f''' III on the keyless recorder. Almost impossible to tongue.

g'''

I. 1̲ 2 4 5 7

The most important fingering for this note, particularly on the bell-keyed recorder. It may be played very softly, with the assistance of 1'' and 2̲. Useful in conjunction with fingerings involving the closure of the bell, including b♭''' I, a''' I, f#''' I, f''' I, and e''' II. This fingering tends towards sharpness on keyless and compromise recorders, and can be flattened by the addition of (½)8.

II. 1̲ 2 (3) 4 6 8

Sweeter than I and at least as important on the keyless recorder, on which it is useful next to f#''' VI. The addition of 3 changes the pitch and minimizes the audibility of the lower attendant sound. However, 3 should be left open in slurred leaps from below.

III. <u>1</u> or 1, 3 4 5 7 8

Somewhat sharp. Especially useful on the keyless recorder, as, for example, for slurs to and from f‴ III. Complete closure of 1 makes this fingering louder and fuller. It may be softened by 1″, <u>3</u>, and <u>4</u>.

IV. <u>1 2 3</u> 5 (½)8

The sweetest and softest of all fingerings for g‴. Also useful for wide slurs from below. Half-stopping of 8 sweetens this fingering still further, but interferes with its ease of speech in slurs from lower notes. Complete closure of 2 and 3 makes it louder. Useful in conjunction with a♭‴ II.

V. <u>1 2 3</u> 5 7 (½)8

An inferior variant of IV, of theoretical interest only.

VI. <u>1</u> 3 4 5 6 (7) 8

Useful for a trill with a♭‴ I, although this trill is better when taken with a♭‴ II and g‴ IV.

VII. <u>1</u> 2 4 X

Useful in conjunction with an f‴ I lower neighbor in quick passages (in which case 4 should usually be left closed for f‴). This fingering generally benefits from 1″ and <u>2</u>.

VIII. <u>1</u> 2 4 5 6 7

The trill with f‴ is best made by means of this variant of I, and f‴ I. Note that the g‴-f‴ trill is impossible to execute on the keyless recorder.

g''' VIII is also useful as a loud fingering, especially with 1 completely closed.

IX. 1̲ 2 4 6 7   See f''' II.

g♯''''-a♭'''

I. 1″ 3 4

Nominally the normal fingering, mainly on account of its simplicity. Often somewhat flat and harsh, particularly on the bell-keyed recorder. Usually benefits from 3̲ and even 4̲ A loud fingering.

II. 1″ 2̲ 3 (½)8

Sweeter and purer than I, especially with ½8, which, however, sometimes interferes with its ease of speech in slurs from below. A soft fingering. Especially useful in conjunction with g''' IV.

III. 1″ 2̲ 3 7 (½)8 ⎫
                    ⎬
IV. 1″ 2 3   ⎭

These inferior derivatives of II are of mainly theoretical significance. III does not speak as readily as II in slurs from below. IV is sharp and edgy.

a'''

I. 1″ 3 4 6 (½)7 X

The best fingering. Tends to be flat, a fault which can be corrected by 3̲ and, some-

times, by 4. Complete closure
of 7 makes this a loud fingering; 3 and 4 make it a soft one.

II. 2 3 4 6 7 X

Superfluous and impractical,
unless the bell key is not covering properly. Useful as a
test for the operation of the
key. (See p. 9.)

III. 1 2 3 4 5 6 7 X

Soft and veiled. Of little practical use.

IV. 1″ 3

To be avoided whenever possible. May be used on the keyless recorder if there is no opportunity to stop the bell with
the knee.

a♯′′′-b♭′′′

I. 1″ 2 3 6 X

Usually the best, particularly
in slurs from below.

II. 1″ 2 3 5 6 X

Softer and sweeter than I, but
does not speak as readily,
particularly in slurs from
below.

III. 1 2 3 4 (5) 6 7 ½8

IV. 1 2 3 4 5 6 8

To be avoided whenever possible. May be used on the keyless recorder when there is no
time to stop the bell with the
knee. IV is sharp, but somewhat less harsh than III; III
is better in tune than IV.

b'''

I. 1″ <u>2</u> 3 5 7   The best fingering.

II. <u>1</u> 2 3 5 6   Useful only as a loud finger-
                                       ing, and for the trill with
                                       c′′′′ IV.

III. 1″ <u>2</u> 3 6   For rapid alternations with
                                       b″ I. Somewhat flat.

IV. 1″ 2 3 5   Of mostly theoretical inter-
                                       est. Sharp.

c′′′′

I. 1″ <u>2</u> 5   The standard fingering for
                                       moderately quick and rapid
                                       passages. Harsh and flat.

II. <u>1</u> 2 3 4 Shade Window   Best in quality. To be used
                                       whenever time and circum-
                                       stances permit. Shading of the
                                       window is accomplished by
                                       cupping the right hand over
                                       the window-like aperture just
                                       below the mouthpiece.

III. 1″ 2 3 5 7 8 X   Better than I, but not as good
                                       as II. Awkward, unless a long
                                       bell key for the left-hand lit-
                                       tle finger is provided.

IV. <u>1</u> 2 3   For the trill with b′′′ II, and
                                       as a very loud fingering.

c#'''' -db''''

I. 1″ 2 4 7 X

This and other notes of the acute registers are of very little practical use, on account of their shrillness and inferior quality. They may, however, be used effectively as peaks of arpeggiated figures, or as sustained notes in orchestral *tutti* passages. c#''''-db'''' is actually somewhat less harsh and impure than c'''' I.

d''''

I. 1 2 4 6

Shrill and impure.

d#''''-eb''''

I. 1 2 3 4 Shade Window

Surprisingly good. I have been unable to discover any conventional fingering for this note.

e''''

I. 1″ 2 3 5 7 X

2 and/or 3 are sometimes necessary. Not too bad, all things considered.

f''''

I. 1″ 2̲ 3 (½)7

Relatively easy to produce, but shrill.

$f^{\#''''}$-$g^{b''''}$

I. 1″ 2̲ 4 6 X̲

The notes above f'''' are of theoretical interest only.

g''''

I. 1̲ 2 3 4 Cover Window

Covering the window resembles shading the window, except that the palm of the right hand is allowed to touch the window.

$g^{\#''''}$-$a^{b''''}$

I. 1″ 2̲ 3 5 7 X̲

Very difficult to produce.

a''''

I. (1̲ 2 3 4) Cover Window

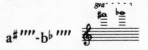

$a^{\#''''}$-$b^{b''''}$

I. 1″ 3̲ 4̲ 5 7 X̲

Almost impossible to obtain.